GOVERNMENT PROCEDURES AND OPERATIONS

MODERNIZING U.S. INSURANCE REGULATION AND THE ROLE OF GLOBAL REINSURANCE MARKETS

GOVERNMENT PROCEDURES AND OPERATIONS

Additional books in this series can be found on Nova's website under the Series tab.

Additional e-books in this series can be found on Nova's website under the e-book tab.

GOVERNMENT PROCEDURES AND OPERATIONS

MODERNIZING U.S. INSURANCE REGULATION AND THE ROLE OF GLOBAL REINSURANCE MARKETS

WILLARD VASQUEZ
EDITOR

nova publishers
New York

Library of Congress Cataloging-in-Publication Data

ISBN: 978-1-63484-338-6

Published by Nova Science Publishers, Inc. † New York

CONTENTS

PREFACE

The insurance sector is a significant part of the U.S. economy (with one estimate putting it at 7 percent of GDP) and an essential asset protection tool for American families and businesses. This book details strengths and weaknesses of current insurance regulatory systems (prudential and marketplace), providing considerations for determining where and how to modernize, and offering a way forward to increase the effectiveness of insurance oversight in the United States. Insurers operating in the United States rely on reinsurers, both foreign and domestic, to support the issuance of new policies, to minimize fluctuations in loss experience, and to limit and diversify individual and portfolio risks, particularly in the case of catastrophes and natural disasters. This book also summarizes the history of reinsurance as a product and an industry, and outlines the various important functions of reinsurance. The book emphasizes that global reinsurers are vital to U.S. insurers and thus important for the general economic prosperity of the United States, including through enhanced availability and affordability of insurance.

In: Modernizing U.S. Insurance Regulation … ISBN: 978-1-63484-338-6
Editor: Willard Vasquez

Chapter 1

HOW TO MODERNIZE AND IMPROVE THE SYSTEM OF INSURANCE REGULATION IN THE UNITED STATES*

Federal Insurance Office

GLOSSARY OF ACRONYMS

Actuarial Guideline 38	AG 38
AIG Financial Products	AIG FP
AIG Securities Lending Corporation	AIGSLC
American Council of Life Insurers	ACLI
American International Group, Inc	AIG
Board of Governors of the Federal Reserve System	Federal Reserve
California Earthquake Authority	Authority
Capital Purchase Program	CPP
Commercial Paper Funding Facility	CPFF
Common Framework for the Supervision of Internationally Active Insurance Groups	ComFrame
Consumer Financial Protection Bureau	CFPB
Council of Insurance Agents and Brokers	CIAB
Credit Default Swap	CDS

* This is an edited, reformatted and augmented version of a report issued by the U.S. Department of the Treasury, December 2013.

Credit Rating Agencies	CRAs
Defense of Marriage Act	DOMA
Department of Housing and Urban Development	HUD
Department of the Treasury	Treasury
Dodd-Frank Wall Street Reform and Consumer Protection Act of 2010	Dodd-Frank Act
European Insurance and Occupational Pensions Authority	EIOPA
European Union	EU
Federal Deposit Insurance Corporation	FDIC
Federal Emergency Management Agency	FEMA
Federal Insurance Office	FIO
Federal Insurance Office Act of 2010	FIO Act
Financial Analysis Working Group	FAWG
Financial Stability Assessment Program	FSAP
Financial Stability Board	FSB
Financial Stability Committee	FSC
Financial Stability Oversight Council	Council
Global Receivership Information Database	GRID
Global Systemically Important Insurers	G-SIIs
Government Accountability Office	GAO
Government Sponsored Enterprises	GSEs
Gramm-Leach-Bliley Act	GLBA
International Association of Insurance Supervisors	IAIS
International Monetary Fund	IMF
Interstate Insurance Product Regulation Commission	IIPRC
Life and Health	L/H
National Association of Insurance Commissioners	NAIC
NAIC Credit for Reinsurance Model Law and Regulation	Model Collateral Law
NAIC Financial Regulation Standards Accreditation Program	Accreditation Program
NAIC Model Insurance Holding Company System Regulatory Act and Regulation	Holding Company Model Act
NAIC Suitability in Annuity Transactions	

Model Regulation	Model Suitability Regulation
National Association of Registered Agents and Brokers	NARAB
National Conference of Insurance Guaranty Funds	NCIGF
National Flood Insurance Program	NFIP
National Insurance Producer Registry	NIPR
National Organization of Life & Health Insurance Guaranty Associations	NOLHGA
New York Department of Financial Services	NYDFS
Non-admitted and Reinsurance Reform Act	NRRA
Office of Thrift Supervision	OTS
Own Risk and Solvency Assessment	ORSA
Principles Based Reserving	PBR
Producer Licensing Model Act	PLMA
Property and Casualty	P/C
Qualified Financial Contracts	QFCs
Quantitative Capital Standard	QCS
Residential Mortgage Backed Securities	RMBS
Risk-based capital	RBC
Secretary of the Treasury	Secretary
Securities and Exchange Commission	SEC
Securities Valuation Office	SVO
Solvency Modernization Initiative	SMI
Special Purpose Vehicle	SPV
Standard Valuation Law	SVL
Statutory accounting principles	SAP
State Modernization and Regulatory Transparency Act	SMART Act
System for Electronic Rate and Form Filing	SERFF
Term Asset-Backed Auction Loan Facility	TALF
Terrorism Risk Insurance Act	TRIA
United States Trade Representative	USTR
Value at Risk	VaR

I. INTRODUCTION

By any measure, insurance is a significant sector of the U.S. economy. Insurance premiums in the life and health (L/H) and property and casualty (P/C) insurance sectors totaled more than $1.1 trillion in 2012,[1] or approximately 7 percent of gross domestic product.[2] In the United States, insurers directly employ approximately 2.3 million people, or 1.7 percent of nonfarm payrolls.[3] More than 2.3 million licensed insurance agents and brokers hold more than 6 million licenses.[4] Moreover, as of year-end 2012, the L/H and P/C sectors reported $7.3 trillion in total assets[5] – roughly half the size of total assets held by insured depository institutions.[6] Of the $7.3 trillion in total assets, $6.8 trillion were invested assets.[7]

The business of insurance in the United States is primarily regulated at the state level. Insurance laws are enacted by state legislators and governors and are implemented and enforced by state regulators. Broadly speaking, state regulation is divided into prudential regulation (frequently referred to as "solvency" regulation) and marketplace regulation. Prudential regulation consists of oversight of an insurer's financial condition and its ability to satisfy policyholder claims. Marketplace regulation governs an insurer's business conduct, such as the pricing of premiums, advertising, minimum standards governing the terms of insurance policies, licensing of insurance agents and brokers (producers), together with general issues of consumer protection and access to insurance.

Although reforms to solvency and marketplace regulation are continually discussed, for over a century a centerpiece of the debate among policymakers and industry leaders over modernizing insurance regulation has been the extent to which the federal government should be involved in insurance regulation. These conversations have generally focused on the question of whether a state-based system can answer the regulatory demands of a national, and increasingly global, insurance market. Proponents of modernizing insurance regulation through federal involvement have noted that the current state-based system does not impose the uniformity necessary for the U.S. insurance market to function efficiently. They explain that state regulation is often duplicative or inconsistent, that the multiplicity of jurisdictions makes state regulators more prone to "capture," and that differences in standards between the states provide opportunities for arbitrage, if not a race to the bottom. Moreover, proponents of federal involvement contend that limitations on the jurisdictional reach of states' legal authority impede effective regulation of entities whose businesses span multiple jurisdictions and sectors.

Those who favor continuation of the current regime of state regulation counter that much of the business of insurance is local in nature and generally does not lend itself to uniform national regulation, and that states are better positioned to respond to consumer complaints. They add that mechanisms for cooperation and achieving uniformity already exist among the states, and that a state-based system provides better opportunities for experimentation so that the best ideas developed in one jurisdiction can be adopted and replicated in others. They also assert that, by and large, state regulation works well.

By drawing attention to the supervision of diversified complex financial institutions such as American International Group, Inc. (AIG), the financial crisis added another dimension to the debate on regulating the insurance industry. The crisis demonstrated that insurers, many of which are large, complex, and global in reach, are integrated into the broader U.S. financial system and that insurers operating within a group may engage in practices that can cause or transmit severe distress to and through the financial system. AIG's near collapse revealed that, despite having several functional regulators, a single regulator did not exercise the responsibility for understanding and supervising the enterprise as a whole.[8] The damage to the broader economy and to the financial system caused by the financial crisis underscored the need to supervise firms on a consolidated basis, to improve safety and soundness standards so as to make firms less susceptible to financial shocks, and to better understand and regulate interconnections between financial companies.[9]

As part of the federal government's response to the financial crisis, Congress passed and President Obama signed into law the Dodd-Frank Wall Street Reform and Consumer Protection Act (Dodd-Frank Act) (Pub. L. 111-203) in July 2010. The Dodd-Frank Act established the Financial Stability Oversight Council (Council), which has the responsibility for monitoring emerging risks to the U.S. financial system and has the authority to determine that nonbank financial companies shall be subject to supervision by the Board of Governors of the Federal Reserve System (Federal Reserve) and prudential standards. Subtitle A of Title V of the Dodd-Frank Act, entitled the Federal Insurance Office Act of 2010 (31 U.S.C. §§ 313-14) (FIO Act), established the Federal Insurance Office (FIO) in the U.S. Department of the Treasury (Treasury). The statute provides FIO with the following authorities:

1) Monitor all aspects of the insurance industry, including identifying issues or gaps in the regulation of insurers that could contribute to a systemic crisis in the insurance industry or the United States financial system;

2) Monitor the extent to which traditionally underserved communities and consumers, minorities, and low- and moderate-income persons have access to affordable insurance products regarding all lines of insurance, except health insurance;
3) Recommend to the Council that it designate an insurer, including the affiliates of such insurer, as an entity subject to regulation as a nonbank financial company supervised by the Federal Reserve;
4) Assist the Secretary of the Treasury (the Secretary) in administering the Terrorism Insurance Program established in the Treasury under the Terrorism Risk Insurance Act of 2002;
5) Coordinate Federal efforts and develop Federal policy on prudential aspects of international insurance matters, including representing the United States, as appropriate, in the International Association of Insurance Supervisors (IAIS) and assisting the Secretary in negotiating covered agreements;[10]
6) Determine whether State insurance measures are preempted by covered agreements;
7) Consult with the States (including State insurance regulators) regarding insurance matters of national importance and prudential insurance matters of international importance; and
8) Perform such other related duties and authorities as may be assigned to FIO by the Secretary.

In addition, the Dodd-Frank Act assigns certain duties to the Director of FIO. Pursuant to Title I of the Dodd-Frank Act, the Director serves as a nonvoting member of the Council. Under Title II, the affirmative approval of the Director, along with a vote of two-thirds of the Governors of the Federal Reserve, is required before the Secretary may make a determination on whether to seek the appointment of the Federal Deposit Insurance Corporation (FDIC) as receiver of an insurance company.

Title V of the Dodd-Frank Act also requires the FIO Director to "conduct a study and submit a report to Congress on how to modernize and improve the system of insurance regulation in the United States."[11] This Report responds to the Congressional directive.

To support this study and Report, FIO has consulted extensively with various stakeholders. On October 17, 2011, FIO published a notice in the Federal Register asking the public to submit comments on the considerations and factors listed in Title V:

- Systemic risk regulation with respect to insurance.
- Capital standards and the relationship between capital allocation and liabilities, including standards relating to liquidity and duration risk.
- Consumer protection for insurance products and practices, including gaps in State regulation.
- The degree of national uniformity of State insurance regulation.
- The regulation of insurance companies and affiliates on a consolidated basis.
- International coordination of insurance regulation.

In addition, Title V states that the Report must also examine:[12]

- The costs and benefits of potential Federal regulation of insurance across various lines of insurance (except health insurance).
- The feasibility of regulating only certain lines of insurance at the Federal level, while leaving other lines of insurance to be regulated at the State level.
- The ability of any potential Federal regulation or Federal regulators to eliminate or minimize regulatory arbitrage.
- The impact that developments in the regulation of insurance in foreign jurisdictions might have on the potential Federal regulation of insurance.
- The ability of any potential Federal regulation or Federal regulator to provide robust consumer protection for policyholders.
- The potential consequences of subjecting companies to a Federal resolution authority, including the effects of any Federal resolution authority -
    - On the operation of State insurance guaranty fund systems, including the loss of guaranty fund coverage if an insurance company is subject to a Federal resolution authority;
    - On policyholder protection, including the loss of the priority status of policyholder claims over other unsecured general creditor claims;
    - In the case of life insurance companies, on the loss of the special status of separate account assets and separate account liabilities; and
    - On the international competitiveness of insurance companies.

- Such other factors as the Director determines necessary or appropriate, consistent with the principles set forth in the prior paragraph.

FIO received nearly 150 written comments, which are available online at treasury.gov/initiatives/fio. In November and December 2011, FIO had an initial round of consultations with nearly 40 different insurance sector participants, ranging from insurance regulators, to insurers, to consumer advocates. On December 9, 2011, FIO hosted a conference at the Treasury where participants representing the interests of consumers, insurers and reinsurers, producers, and academics discussed regulatory modernization. Topics included marketplace oversight and licensing, international developments, and prudential oversight. FIO's study and consultations continued throughout 2012 and 2013. This Report reflects some of the many issues and topics raised by stakeholders throughout the consultative process, including through written comments, at the Treasury conference, and also through FIO's direct engagement with federal, state, and international supervisors.

Structure of the Report

This Report is divided into five principal sections. Section I, the introduction, presents the recommendations for modernizing insurance regulation in the United States. This discussion also includes a general assessment of whether federal involvement is necessary in the regulation of insurance and, if so, what manner that involvement should take.

Section II describes the history of insurance regulation in the United States, highlighting significant events in its development. The historical perspective helps frame the current debates on modernization by illustrating the continuing debate, raised in different contexts and time periods, as to whether federal or state insurance regulation would best address the need for improved uniformity and oversight. This section begins by discussing the advent of state insurance regulation in the 19th century, key Supreme Court decisions such as *Paul v. Virginia* (1868) and *United States v. South-Eastern Underwriters* (1944), the passage of the McCarran-Ferguson Act in 1945, the reaction of state regulators and Congress to insolvency crises in the 1960s through the early 1990s, and the passage, in 1999, of the GrammLeach-Bliley Act (GLBA). This section also explores state regulators' reaction to

Congressional interest in insurance regulation and outlines recent proposals for federal oversight. It concludes by discussing the financial crisis, reforms enacted under the Dodd-Frank Act, and the creation of FIO.

Section III presents the analysis underlying the recommendations regarding prudential oversight issues. It reviews the framework by which insurers are evaluated and regulated for solvency as these topics are currently being discussed by the U.S. and the international regulatory communities, including the European Union (EU) and the IAIS. More specifically, this section analyzes the approaches state regulators use to assess an insurer's capital adequacy, together with discretionary practices and emerging issues on reserving and the regulation of captives. This section also discusses corporate governance matters and group supervision in the context of national and international reforms. Finally, this section evaluates current approaches to insurer resolution and guaranty fund processes.

Section IV presents the analysis supporting the recommendations concerning marketplace oversight, focusing on market and consumer issues that have been the subject of the recurring debate on national regulatory uniformity. Some of the principal topics in this area are: (1) multi-state licensing for insurance producers; (2) the state-based insurance product approval processes; (3) examinations of an insurer's market conduct; (4) rate regulation; and (5) insurance scoring and risk classification practices for personal lines insurance consumers. This section also reviews the states' regulatory treatment of insurance lines affected by natural catastrophes, the accessibility of insurance to Native American communities, collection of taxes for multi-state surplus lines placements, and suitability standards for the sale of annuity products.

Section V discusses insurance modernization in the context of basic principles of regulatory reform. The Report comprehensively addresses all of the statutory considerations and factors, but not in a serial or individual manner.

Recommendations for Modernization of Insurance Regulation in the United States

For over a century, the debate over reform of insurance regulation in the United States has focused largely on the practical and legal limitations of the state-based insurance regulatory system. The absence of uniformity in the U.S. insurance regulatory system creates inefficiencies and burdens for consumers, insurers, and the international community. For example, per dollar of premium, the costs of the state-based insurance regulatory system are approximately 6.8 times greater for an insurer operating in the United States than for an insurer operating in the United Kingdom, and increase costs for P/C insurers by $7.2 billion annually and for life insurers by $5.7 billion annually.[13] The need for uniformity and the realities of globally active, diversified financial firms compel the conclusion that federal involvement of some kind in insurance regulation is necessary. Regulation at the federal level would improve uniformity, efficiency, and consistency, and it would address concerns with uniform supervision of insurance firms with national and global activities.

The increasingly international dimension of the insurance marketplace, in and of itself, is also an important consideration. U.S. firms are not the only ones with a global reach. Non-U.S. firms have significantly expanded market share around the world, including in the U.S. direct and reinsurance markets, a trend that likely will continue because of the size of the U.S. insurance market. Insurance regulatory issues will increasingly require international attention and cooperation. The federal government's predominant role in foreign affairs is one reason for the necessity of a federal presence in insurance regulation. It would be much less costly, much less prone to arbitrage, and much easier to negotiate internationally for more efficient and effective oversight of the insurance sector if U.S. insurance regulation had greater uniformity and predictability.

The limitations inherent in a state-based system of insurance regulation, however, do not necessarily imply that the ideal solution would be for the federal government to displace state regulation completely. The business of insurance involves offering many products that are tailored for and delivered at a local level. For the most part, effective delivery of the product will require local knowledge and relationships, and local regulation. Moreover, establishing a new federal agency to regulate all or part of the $7.3 trillion insurance sector would be a significant undertaking. The personnel, resources, and institutional expertise needed to execute such an endeavor at a professional and rigorous level would, of necessity, require an unequivocal commitment from the legislative and executive branches of the U.S. government.

In light of these considerations, this Report concludes that the proper formulation of the debate at present is not whether insurance regulation should be state or federal, but whether there are areas in which federal involvement in regulation under the state-based system is warranted. Reframed in this manner, the basic question with respect to reforming any aspect of insurance should be whether federal involvement is warranted at this time and, if so, in what areas. The necessity for federal involvement should depend on assessment of questions such as whether states can take measures to regulate effectively and with uniformity, the degree of the national or federal interest, and the nexus of the issues and the firms with the global marketplace.

If the answer to the first inquiry is that federal involvement is warranted, the inquiry then turns to what kind of federal involvement would best provide for attaining the policy objectives. Federal involvement can take many forms, ranging from direct regulation to standard-setting or operating a program that supports or replaces an otherwise failed insurance market. In all events, federal involvement should be targeted to areas in which that involvement would solve problems resulting from the legal and practical limitations of regulation by states, such as the need for uniformity or the need for a federal voice in U.S. interactions with international authorities.

In light of the foregoing, FIO believes that, in the short term, the U.S. system of insurance regulation can be modernized and improved by a combination of steps by the states and certain actions by the federal government. The recommendations are as follows.

Areas of Near-Term Reform for the States

Capital Adequacy and Safety/Soundness

1) For material solvency oversight decisions of a discretionary nature, states should develop and implement a process that obligates the appropriate state regulator to first obtain the consent of regulators from other states in which the subject insurer operates.
2) To improve consistency of solvency oversight, states should establish an independent, third-party review mechanism for the National Association of Insurance Commissioners Financial Regulation Standards Accreditation Program.
3) States should develop a uniform and transparent solvency oversight regime for the transfer of risk to reinsurance captives.
4) State-based solvency oversight and capital adequacy regimes should converge toward best practices and uniform standards.
5) States should move forward cautiously with the implementation of principles-based reserving and condition it upon: (1) the establishment of consistent, binding guidelines to govern regulatory practices that

determine whether a domestic insurer complies with accounting and solvency requirements; and (2) attracting and retaining supervisory resources and developing uniform guidelines to monitor supervisory review of principles-based reserving.

6) States should develop corporate governance principles that impose character and fitness expectations on directors and officers appropriate to the size and complexity of the insurer.
7) In the absence of direct federal authority over an insurance group holding company, states should continue to develop approaches to group supervision and address the shortcomings of solo entity supervision.
8) State regulators should build toward effective group supervision by continued attention to supervisory colleges.

Reform of Insurer Resolution Practices

9) States should: (1) adopt a uniform approach to address the closing out and netting of qualified contracts with counterparties; and (2) develop requirements for transparent financial reporting regarding the administration of a receivership estate.
10) States should adopt and implement uniform policyholder recovery rules so that policyholders, irrespective of where they reside, receive the same maximum benefits from guaranty funds.

Marketplace Regulation

11) States should assess whether or in what manner marital status is an appropriate underwriting or rating consideration.
12) State-based insurance product approval processes should be improved by securing the participation of every state in the Interstate Insurance Product Regulation Commission (IIPRC) and by expanding the products subject to approval by the IIPRC. State regulators should pursue the development of nationally standardized forms and terms, or an interstate compact, to further streamline and improve the regulation of commercial lines.
13) In order to fairly protect consumers in all parts of the United States, every state should adopt and enforce the National Association of Insurance Commissioners Suitability in Annuities Transactions Model Regulation.
14) States should reform market conduct examination and oversight practices and: (1) require state regulators to perform market conduct

examinations consistent with the National Association of Insurance Commissioners Market Regulation Handbook; (2) seek information from other regulators before issuing a request to an insurer; (3) develop standards and protocols for contract market conduct examiners; and (4) develop a list of approved contract examiners based on objective qualification standards.

15) States should monitor the impact of different rate regulation regimes on various markets in order to identify rate-related regulatory practices that best foster competitive markets for personal lines insurance consumers.
16) States should develop standards for the appropriate use of data for the pricing of personal lines insurance.
17) States should extend regulatory oversight to vendors that provide insurance score products to insurers.
18) States should identify, adopt, and implement best practices to mitigate losses from natural catastrophes.

Areas for Direct Federal Involvement in Regulation

1) Federal standards and oversight for mortgage insurers should be developed and implemented.
2) To afford nationally uniform treatment of reinsurers, FIO recommends that Treasury and the United States Trade Representative pursue a covered agreement for reinsurance collateral requirements based on the National Association of Insurance Commissioners Credit for Reinsurance Model Law and Regulation.
3) FIO should engage in supervisory colleges to monitor financial stability and identify issues or gaps in the regulation of large national and internationally active insurers.
4) The National Association of Registered Agents and Brokers Reform Act of 2013 should be adopted and its implementation monitored by FIO.
5) FIO will convene and work with federal agencies, state regulators, and other interested parties to develop personal auto insurance policies for U.S. military personnel enforceable across state lines.
6) FIO will work with state regulators to establish pilot programs for rate regulation that seek to maximize the number of insurers offering personal lines products.

7) FIO will study and report on the manner in which personal information is used for insurance pricing and coverage purposes.
8) FIO will consult with Tribal leaders to identify alternatives to improve the accessibility and affordability of insurance on sovereign Native American and Tribal lands.
9) FIO will continue to monitor state progress on implementation of Subtitle B of Title V of the Dodd-Frank Act, which requires states to simplify the collection of surplus lines taxes, and determine whether federal action may be warranted in the near term.

Potential Federal Solutions to States' Failure to Modernize and Improve

As detailed further in this Report, many of the areas for which FIO recommends that there be reform of the state regulatory system relate to subject matter areas in which the states already have been working to make changes. For a variety of reasons, however, progress has been uneven despite the absence of any dispute about the need for change. As a result, should the states fail to accomplish necessary modernization reforms in the near term, Congress should strongly consider direct federal involvement.

The precise manner of federal involvement is a matter for Congress to determine. Recent experience suggests that proposals for federal involvement have fallen into two paradigms: (1) the federal government serving as a coordinating body that also adopts national rules and standards that would preempt state law, but that would leave direct enforcement of the rules and standards to the states; and (2) direct federal regulation of selected areas or aspects of the insurance industry, whether it be oversight of one element of the distribution chain (*e.g.*, multi-state producer licensing) or a particular line of insurance.

Federal Standards Implemented by the States

The first paradigm is for the federal government to serve as a coordinating and facilitating body to assist states with developing national standards and rules. One example of this approach occurred in 1990, when Congress mandated the development of standard benefit designs for Medicare supplement policies. This approach imposed uniform product design on so-called "Medi-gap" policies, thereby enabling consumers to comparison shop. Under this approach, Congress permitted the states to develop the product standards promulgated as regulation by the U.S. Department of Health and Human Services Center for Medicare and Medicaid Services.

Another example is the National Association of Registered Agents and Brokers Reform Act of 2013 (NARAB II), which is presently under consideration by Congress. Under NARAB II, a commission would be established and guided by a board comprised of state regulators and producers. The National Association of Registered Agents and Brokers (NARAB) would be responsible for issuing multi-state licenses to producers which would preempt the application of any state law or regulation for purposes of licensing and continuing education. Standards will be established, in part, by state regulators, and producers will benefit from one centralized licensing location and process.

Other reform proposals have resembled the foregoing examples of federal/state collaboration. Congress explored one such approach in 2004, when two members of Congress offered a discussion draft known as the "State Modernization and Regulatory Transparency Act," or the "SMART Act." This discussion draft put forth a comprehensive insurance reform proposal that would have provided for the development of national standards and coordinated regulation. It proposed that uniform standards would be enforced at the state level. While the states would develop the uniform standard, each uniformity requirement included an enforcement mechanism to incentivize state participation. For example, failure to streamline licensing for producers would result in preemption of the law of the state that failed to adopt the uniformity standard. This discussion draft, if introduced and adopted, would have required uniform standards for issues that remain a challenge today: producer licensing, product approval, and surplus lines tax remittance, among others.

One proposed reform has been to adopt a "state passport system."[14] In this scenario, Congress would establish a national standard, or would defer rulemaking on an appropriate topic to an administrative agency, and failure by the states to implement an appropriate national standard would then result in federal preemption. Another version of the national passport approach would authorize FIO, for example, to evaluate state regulatory standards and identify best practices or national standards based on consensus of the states. If FIO surveys state regulatory practices, whether by mandate or choice, FIO could determine whether a satisfactory level of uniformity exists and promulgate that standard as a national target.

Another variant of federal standard-setting is the "federal tools" concept, whereby Congress enacts a regulatory standard and requires the states to develop, adopt, and implement regulation consistent with the standard. A "tools" bill typically requires state action within a limited period of time. In the absence of appropriate state action, or action by a defined number of states, then the federal law preempts the law in those states that have failed to act.

Federal standard-setting schemes can have shortcomings. First, if the legislation delegates a vague standard or objective to the states, it is unlikely to improve uniformity and efficiency as intended. Second, if the legislation contemplates an opt-in by the states, the probability that all states would opt-in may be small.

Thus, while bills to establish federal standards appear to promote incremental improvement on targeted areas, such legislation must specify standards, processes, and a deadline in order to minimize or eliminate the prospect of variance among the states. This experience points to a more general challenge for federal involvement as a standard-setter. Standards themselves may impose a degree of uniformity. However, application of those standards is equally important to imposing uniformity and consistency. Therefore, if federal involvement is to occur through standard-setting, it should be accompanied by mechanisms designed to enhance uniform implementation of the standards through proper, consistent enforcement.

Direct Federal Regulation

One manner of providing for uniform application of rules is to authorize the federal government itself to directly enforce federally-developed and adopted standards and rules. A number of proposals would have subjected much, if not the entirety, of insurance regulation to direct federal oversight. The underlying concept is that the federal government would act not just as standard-setter or rule-maker, but also as regulator and enforcer. Many view this as an essential objective of modernization due to the size and globalization of the insurance sector and its importance to the national economy. Others assert that the federal government need not regulate the entire insurance business, but only certain aspects of it.

For example, one approach would be to adopt federal regulation for those insurance firms that exceed thresholds of size, scale, and complexity, or those that have national or global business operations. Another approach, which has been a focus of prior proposals, is an optional federal charter, whereby those firms that opt for federal charters would be subject to federal regulation. Federal licensing and regulation of insurers, however, could be defined by the terms of eligibility. As proposed in the National Insurance Act of 2007 and the National Insurance Consumer Protection Act of 2009, the optional federal charter approach would leave to insurers the choice to adopt a federal charter and, therefore, to be regulated by the federal government or by the states.[15] Yet another approach would be a combination of the first two, where, in general, firms would have an option to adopt a federal charter, but that federal regulation for certain large, globally active firms would be mandatory.

II. A Brief History of the Regulation of the United States Insurance Industry

Early Era of Insurance Regulation and the Limitation on Federal Authority

States first created corporate insurance companies in the late 18th century by enacting individual statutes or charters specific to each insurer. To supervise the activities of a growing industry, in 1851, New Hampshire appointed the first state insurance commissioner. A number of states followed soon thereafter. By 1871, each of the then-36 states had an insurance regulator.

There was evidence early that multistate activity by insurers could create tension with the state-based regulatory regimes. An early manifestation was the case of *Paul v. Virginia*, 75 U.S. 168 (1868). Several New York insurers had hired an agent to sell policies in Virginia, but because the insurers refused to deposit the licensing bond required by Virginia law, Virginia denied the agent a license. When the agent nevertheless sold policies, he was convicted for violating Virginia law. The New York insurers argued to the Supreme Court that the Virginia law was unconstitutional, in part as a violation of the Commerce Clause of the Constitution. The Court rejected the argument, and stated that the business of insurance was not a transaction of interstate commerce, thus placing insurance beyond the authority of the federal government to regulate. Accordingly, the ruling effectively established the states as regulators of the insurance sector.

The Court's decision did not eliminate multistate activity and, with multistate activity, there was recognition of the need for uniformity of rules in different states. The insurance industry and state regulators began to seek ways to promote coordination between states. In 1871, George W. Miller, New York's superintendent of insurance, invited the insurance commissioners from all 36 states to participate in a meeting to discuss insurance regulation. Representatives from 19 states attended the inaugural meeting of the association known today as the National Association of Insurance Commissioners (NAIC). The importance of uniformity was expressed at that meeting:

> In a session "remarkable for its harmony," the commissioners are now "fully prepared to go before their various legislative committees with recommendations for a system of insurance law which shall be the same in all states—not reciprocal, but identical; not retaliatory, but uniform. That repeated consultation and future concert of action will eventuate in the removal of discriminating and oppressive statutes which now disgrace our codes, and that the companies and the public will both be largely benefited, we have no manner of doubt."[16]

Box 1: The National Association of Insurance Commissioners (NAIC)

The NAIC is a voluntary organization that consists of the chief insurance regulatory officials of the 50 states, the District of Columbia, America Samoa, Guam, Puerto Rico, the U.S. Virgin Islands, and the Northern Mariana Islands. Originally formed in 1871, the NAIC reorganized in 1999 as a non-profit corporation under the general corporate laws of the State of Delaware and is a 501(c) (3) tax exempt organization.

The NAIC itself is an association, not a regulator or government entity. Accordingly, public sect( )1 requirements do not govern the NAIC's administration, including employment, compensation, and procurement practices. As a private 501(c) (3) organization, the NAIC does not have authority to bind any state or state official to any law, policy, or practice, nor does it have the authority to speak for the United States. Similarly, the NAIC's 501(c) (3) status defines the extent to which it may engage in political and lobbying activities.

Purposes and Functions

The NAIC describes in its 2012 Annual Report the organization's function as a forum through which state regulators develop model laws and regulations:

"The NAIC provides its members with a national forum for discussing common issues and interests, as well as for working cooperatively on regulatory matters that transcend the boundaries of their own jurisdictions. Collectively, commissioners work to develop model legislation, rules, regulations and white papers to coordinate regulatory policy.

The overriding objective is to protect consumers and help maintain the financial stability of the insurance marketplace."

Development of a model law proceeds in a number of stages, but must first be authorized by the Executive Committee, the managing committee of the NAIC. A number of qualifying criteria must be met before development of a model law is undertaken, including both: (1) the need for a national standard and uniformity among the states on the relevant policy issue and (2) the commitment among state regulators to support and implement a model law. Once a model law goes through the appropriate committees for review, its adoption by the NAIC occurs at a plenary session and requires a favorable vote of two-thirds of the NAIC members then attending. Model laws are generally not adopted unifoiinly and only become effective in a particular state if and when enacted by that state's legislature.

The NAIC also provides support services to assist states in implementing regulations. The level of state participation and use of each of these products and tools vary. Five such NAIC services are:

- Interstate Insurance Product Regulation Commission (IIPRC), which offers a centralized life insurance product approval process for 41 states;
- National Insurance Producer Registry (NIPR), which provides a national electronic databa',e of licensed insurance producers;
- System for Electronic Rate and Form Filings (SERFF), which provides an electronic form and rate filing system for insurance products;
- State Based Systems, which offers on-line registration for producers; and,
- Online Premium Tax for Insurance, which allows for payment of premium taxes for multistate placements.

Structure and Budget

The NAIC's 2013 approved budget includes total revenues of $80.0 million, expenses of $81.2 million, and a total unrestricted net asset balance of $83.3 million. Revenue supporting the NAIC budget is derived from three primary sources: database filing fees paid by the insurance industry in connection with required statutory filings ($26.8 million, or 33.5 percent of budgeted revenues); sales of publications and insurance data products ($19.5 million, or 24.4 percent); and fees paid by the insurance industry for other services provided by the NAIC to satisfy state regulatory requirements ($21.1 million, or 26.3 percent). The data that is included in NAIC products is taken from an insurance sector database that has been populated by data in reports filed with the NAIC by insurers pursuant to state regulatory requirements. State regulators also contribute $2.3 million (2.9 percent) through membership assessments. For 2013, the NAIC budget authorizes employment of up to 462 full-time equivalent positions across its three offices: the Executive Office in Washington, D.C.; the Capital Markets and Investments Office in New York, New York; and the Central Office in Kansas City, Missouri.

In addition to the Plenary and Executive Committees, the NAIC has seven major committees, each of which is responsible for particular areas of regulatory concern. A major committee may have task forces — as well as working groups and sub-working groups — that address specific issues. The seven major committees are:

- Life Insurance and Annuities (A) Committee
- Health and Managed Care (B) Committee
- Property and Casualty (C) Committee
- Market Regulation and Consumer Affairs (D) Committee
- Financial Condition (E) Committee
- Financial Regulation Standards and Accreditation (F) Committee
- International Insurance Relations (G) Committee

Early Calls for Federal Regulation of Insurance

The perceived state of the insurance industry in the early years of the 20th century sparked a debate about a potential federal role in insurance regulation. In the early 20th century, highly publicized reports and accusations of market manipulation and fraud associated with insurers prompted the New York State legislature, for example, to investigate the business practices of some of the largest life insurers. The results of the investigation documented abuses by life insurers, including stock market manipulation, falsified records to hide campaign contributions, and officers using company funds for personal use.[17] Against this background, President Theodore Roosevelt spoke in favor of federal insurance regulation in his Annual Address to Congress in 1904. Discussing the strains on the state regulatory system through the growth of the insurance industry, he justified federal intervention by stating that the insurance business is "national and not local in its application," and "involves a multitude of transactions among the people of the different States and between American companies and foreign governments."'

In 1905, Senator John Dryden of New Jersey, founder and president of the Prudential Life Insurance Company, introduced a bill to implement President Roosevelt's recommendation for the federal regulation of insurance by creating a "Bureau of Insurance" in the Department of Commerce and Labor, which was to be led by a "Comptroller of Insurance" appointed by the President to a four year term. He expanded the justification for federal regulation from combating manipulation and fraud to promoting uniformity and efficiency. Senator Dryden maintained, for example, that his bill would increase security to policyholders, decrease the cost of insurance, and result in "diminution of a vast amount of needless clerical labor to meet the requirements of some fifty different States and Territories and consequent decrease in expense rate."[19] He added, "Whatever may be said in favor of the national regulation of banks and railways applies with equal, if not greater, force in the case of this now universal institution, reaching as it does, all classes and affecting more or less all commercial interests."[20] Thus, Senator Dryden offered many of the arguments that would be repeated in the following decades in favor of federal insurance regulation. Congress did not pass Senator Dryden's proposed bill. Not everyone agreed that a federal solution was warranted. During the same period in which Senator Dryden introduced his legislation, for example, Louis Brandeis, then practicing law in Boston before becoming a Supreme Court Justice, expressed his belief that state regulation was preferable. At the time, he served as counsel to a New England policyholders' committee that was concerned about the potential bankruptcy of Equitable Life Assurance of New York. After undertaking a study of the insurance industry, Brandeis expressed concerns about dishonest and inefficient management, the amount of capital that the large insurers controlled, and the inefficiency of state regulation. He nevertheless favored improving state regulation to replacing it with federal regulation, characterizing Senator's Dryden's proposal as a way to "free the companies from the careful scrutiny ... of the States."[21]

The Case of *South-Eastern Underwriters,* Federal Authority to Regulate Insurance, and the McCarran-Ferguson Act

In 1944, in a reversal of its previous position, the Supreme Court concluded that Congress had the power to regulate insurance transactions across state lines.[22] In so concluding, it echoed the types of arguments made earlier by President Roosevelt and Senator Dryden, noting that insurance, "has become one of the largest and most important branches of commerce," and, "[p]erhaps no modern commercial enterprise directly affects so many persons in all walks of life as does the insurance business."[23]

The case that occasioned the Supreme Court's decision can be traced back to the San Francisco earthquake of 1906, which bankrupted many fire insurers. In the wake of these bankruptcies, a number of states allowed insurers to set premium rates collaboratively, which allowed insurers to avoid competition in pricing premiums. The rationale was that avoiding such competition would prevent a deterioration in insurers' financial condition and, consequently, possible insurer insolvencies. The insurance industry formed panels to collaboratively set rates in states where such rate setting was permitted.

Missouri did not allow collaborative rate setting. Certain fire insurers, however, were found by the United States to be bribing Missouri state officials to permit them to maintain rates in a manner that effectively amounted to rate setting. The United States filed suit alleging that the bribes and the rate setting constituted price fixing by a cartel in violation of the Sherman Antitrust Act. The case was brought against the South-Eastern Underwriters Association, the largest rate-setting bureau, and ultimately was presented to the Supreme Court in 1944. Cases such as *Paul* had raised the question whether a state had the authority to regulate and to tax specific activities of insurers based in other states. The antitrust claim presented in the *South-Eastern Underwriters* case, however, raised the question whether the Commerce Clause of the Constitution granted Congress the power to regulate insurance transactions across state lines. The Court held that insurers were engaged in interstate commerce and concluded that, even though Congress had not specifically included a provision in the Sherman Act to apply to insurance, Congress had the power to include insurers within the scope of federal law.[24]

In 1945, in response to the *South-Eastern Underwriters* decision, Congress passed the McCarran-Ferguson Act[25] to clarify that state laws governing the business of insurance are not invalidated, impaired, or superseded by any federal law unless the federal law specifically relates to the business of insurance.[26] In the Act, Congress stated that, "the continued regulation and taxation by the several States of the business of insurance is in the public interest, and that silence on the part of Congress shall not be construed to impose any barrier to the regulation or taxation of such business by the several states."

The Crises of Insurer Insolvencies, Congressional Reaction, and State Regulatory Responses

A wave of insolvencies among auto insurers in the 1960s rekindled the debate over the adequacy of state regulation and the inadequate level of uniformity in insurance regulation among the states. In the absence of guaranty funds, failure of these auto insurers left policyholders without adequate recourse against the assets of the insolvent insurer. The crisis attracted Congressional attention and, in 1966, prompted a proposal to create a federal guaranty system for insurers, modeled on federal bank deposit insurance.[27] A decade later, in 1976, Senator Edward Brooke introduced the Federal Insurance Act, which would have authorized the federal government to offer optional federal insurance charters, preempting state law, and would also have created a federal guaranty fund.[28] In a parallel effort a few years earlier, in 1969, state regulators, through the NAIC, developed a model guaranty fund act for property and liability insurance and, in 1970, a similar model for life and health insurance. Guaranty funds aimed to improve policyholder protection with an industry-funded, *ex post* claims payment system whereby consumers would receive some contractual benefit despite an insurer's failure. Many states adopted versions of this model legislation.

After another series of insurer insolvencies, this time involving over 50 insurers in the 1980s and 1990s, including the largest life insurer in California at the time, Congress began a more extensive investigation into the adequacy of insurer solvency regulation. The House Committee on Energy and Commerce's Subcommittee on Oversight and Investigations, chaired by Congressman John Dingell, issued a report in 1990 entitled *Failed Promises: Insurance Company Insolvencies*.[29] The report found that, "the present system for regulating the solvency of insurers is seriously deficient" due to rapid and unbridled expansion, underpricing, inadequate oversight, inadequate loss reserves, poor reinsurance transactions, and fraud.[30] In 1992, Chairman Dingell introduced a bill that, if enacted, would have instituted federal regulation of insurer solvency.[31] In 1994, the same subcommittee issued a second report on insurer solvency regimes, entitled *Wishful Thinking: A World View of Insurance Solvency Regulation*.[32] The report stated that, notwithstanding state regulatory efforts to address solvency reform, regulation remained insufficient because state regulators lacked adequate national and international authority.[33] A minority report released by the subcommittee, however, disagreed and stated that it favored "strengthening, not dismantling, the current State regulatory system."[34]

In the aftermath of the *Failed Promises* and *Wishful Thinking* reports, in the 1990s, state regulators, through the NAIC, developed and adopted risk-based capital (RBC) formulae for life, property/casualty and health insurers. At the same time, states developed and adopted a self-accreditation program now known as the Financial Standards and Accreditation Program, a peer review process intended to improve consistency of financial regulation across the state system. Later, in 2001, after several years of development, state regulators codified statutory accounting principles (SAP) in an effort to further policyholder protection.

Recent Proposals for Federal Regulation of Insurance to Promote Uniformity

A number of proposals have been set forth more recently to enact federal legislation to address the inconsistency and absence of uniformity in the state-based system of insurance regulation. An important initial effort occurred in 1999, when Congress passed the GLBA.[35] Although GLBA allowed banks to affiliate with insurers through a federally regulated financial holding company, it preserved the states' authorities to regulate insurance company affiliates. GLBA introduced the possibility of addressing the absence of uniformity in one key area of state regulation, however, when it included the requirement for the creation of NARAB to implement national insurance agent licensing requirements if a majority of the states and territories did not meet a 2002 deadline for reciprocity in producer licensing.[36] In 2002, the state regulators certified that 35 states and territories had satisfied the GLBA requirement, enough to constitute a majority and thereby avoiding the creation of NARAB.[37]

GLBA was the beginning of a series of efforts over the ensuing decade to bring a federal regulatory presence to insurance. Between 2001 and 2006, the House Financial Services Committee held more than a dozen hearings at both the subcommittee and full committee levels on insurance matters at which witnesses discussed issues such as the increasing globalization of the insurance sector and inefficiencies attendant to the lack of uniformity in the state-based system of regulation. Members of Congress also offered legislative solutions. Congressman Michael Oxley and Congressman Richard Baker, for example, released a discussion draft called the State Modernization and Regulatory Transparency Act (SMART Act) in 2004, which proposed that states comply with uniform standards for licensing, market conduct regulation, reinsurance practices, and receivership rules. It also proposed expediting the process of introducing new insurance products to the market and shifting toward a system of market-based rates.[38]

Although the SMART Act would have required significant increases in the degree of uniformity, state regulators' authorities would have been preserved. Other proposals, however, have prescribed more extensive federal regulatory involvement to promote uniform national insurance regulation. For example, a number of bills have called for the creation of an optional federal charter, such as the National Insurance Act of 2007, co-sponsored in the Senate by Senators Tim Johnson and John Sununu, and in the House by Representatives Melissa Bean and Edward Royce.[39] This proposed legislation would have created an optional federal charter for property/casualty and life insurance.[40]

The Executive Branch presented a similar proposal in a 2008 report by the Treasury entitled *Blueprint for a Modernized Financial Regulatory Structure*.[41] Noting that the insurance regulatory system suffered from duplicative, inconsistent, and non-uniform regulation, the report proposed the creation of an optional federal insurance charter as an interim step toward a unified national chartering system. The *Blueprint* also included proposals for federal licensing for insurance producers and the creation of an Office of Insurance Oversight at Treasury.[42] In April 2009, The National Insurance Consumer Protection Act was introduced in the House by Representatives Bean and Royce with the stated purpose of improving uniformity in insurance regulation.[43] The bill proposed a single, optional federal charter for the insurance industry, including insurers, reinsurers, and insurance producers.[44]

In June 2009, the Treasury released *Financial Regulatory Reform: A New Foundation* that recommended the establishment of an Office of National Insurance "to gather information, develop expertise, negotiate international agreements, and coordinate policy in the insurance sector."[45] In this policy statement, the Treasury articulated six principles by which to measure proposals for insurance regulatory reform:

1) Effective systemic risk regulation with respect to insurance.
2) Strong capital standards and appropriate match between capital allocation and liabilities for all insurance companies.
3) Meaningful and consistent consumer protection for insurance products and practices.
4) Increased national uniformity through either a federal charter or effective action by the states.

5) Improve and broaden the regulation of insurance companies and affiliates on a consolidated basis, including those affiliates outside of the traditional insurance business.
6) Increased international coordination. Improvements to our system of insurance regulation should satisfy existing international frameworks, enhance the international competitiveness of the American insurance industry, and expand opportunities for the insurance industry to export its services.

The Financial Crisis

In 2007-2009, the United States faced the most severe financial crisis since the Great Depression. Like other parts of the financial sector, the insurance industry was affected by the crisis in several ways.

One of the most notable events of the crisis was the near-collapse of AIG, which threatened the stability of the entire U.S. financial system. Although MG was principally an insurer, it also conducted other businesses, including a large amount of derivatives trading and securities lending. At the end of 2007, AIG's derivatives book was nearly $2.65 trillion in outstanding notional amounts." While some derivatives were used for hedging in the conduct of AIG's insurance business, its large credit default swap portfolio ($562 billion at the end of 2007)[47] was located in a non-insurance, non-regulated affiliate, and these derivatives proved to be a major source of financial trouble for the firm and the U.S. financial system. Another major source of AIG's losses came from its large securities lending activities which were conducted through both insurance and non-insurance affiliates.

MG owned a thrift and, therefore, AIG's holding company was regulated by the Office of Thrift Supervision (OTS). However, GLBA generally limited the authority of the OTS to supervise state-regulated insurance entities.

In the absence of an effective consolidated supervisor, MG conducted its credit default swap (CDS) business largely outside of regulatory purview and engaged in securities lending activities that had not been previously approved. As it turned out, MG did not have sufficient capital or liquidity to withstand the deterioration in the financial condition of its CDS and securities lending businesses that occurred during the financial *crisis. (See* Box 2.) The experience with MG underscored the importance of consolidated supervision and appropriate prudential standards for certain types of nonbank financial institutions.

Box 2: AIG

Prior to the financial crisis MG was regarded as the world's largest insurance firm with products in nearly every business line and entities domiciled throughout the United States and internationally. AIG's U.S.-based legal insurance entities were subject to state regulatory oversight. Due to the limits of state regulatory authority, the supervisory oversight of AIG's non-insurance operations was completely separate and distinct from oversight of its insurance businesses. While AIG's business ventures developed into complex non-insurance activities, the scope of state regulatory authority was demonstrably inadequate given AIG's size, scale, and complexity.

Credit Default Swaps

MG conducted its CDS business through MG Financial Products (MG FP), which operated in Wilton, Connecticut; London, England; and Paris, France. Despite its locations in Europe, this subsidiary was not regulated by the EU because the EU recognized the U.S. Office of Thrift Supervision as the lead consolidated supervisor, meaning that the EU effectively deferred responsibility for supervision to the OTS. The OTS, however, rarely conducted examinations of MG FP's activities, which included writing about $562 billion of credit default swap protection. In part because of the fair value impairments associated with its CDS business, MG experienced significant margin calls in 2007, was downgraded by the credit rating agencies in 2008, and ultimately, turned to the U.S. federal government to provide exceptional assistance.

Securities Lending

AIG's insurance subsidiaries authorized a non-insurance affiliate, MG Securities Lending Corporation (AIGSLC), to act on behalf of the subsidiaries to loan securities to other financial institutions in exchange for cash collateral. Although state regulators regulated only the MG insurance entities and did not supervise AIGSLC, state regulators did approve the risk parameters that originally guided AIG's securities lending practices. Over time, however, MG deviated from the approved parameters to grow a once-conservative business into a source of material risk to the insurers engaged in the securities lending activity.

In 2005, MG began investing the cash collateral it received through securities lending activities into residential mortgage backed securities (RMBS), which provided a return on investment higher than other securities.' By 2007, approximately 60 percent of AIG's invested securities lending collateral were in RMBS. As the mortgage crisis deepened, credit rating agencies downgraded RMBS from AAA status. The resulting drop in price and tightening liquidity in the underlying market for structured securities was a significant impediment to MG selling its RMBS investments for cash in order to meet collateral calls. In the last two weeks of September 2008 alone, AIG's securities lending counterparties demanded that MG return approximately $24 billion in cash. This problem was exacerbated by the fact that the average maturity of the RMBS securities was materially longer than the average maturity of the securities loans, which often ranged from overnight to 60 days in maturity.

In 2007, state regulators identified the risks associated with AIG's shift from holding cash collateral to investing in RMBS. As of December 2007, securities lending assets and liabilities represented 7 percent and 8.5 percent, respectively, of AIG's consolidated balance sheet. Although numerous life insurers within AIG's corporate structure were involved in securities lending, the actual operations were centralized in AIGSLC.

During the financial crisis, the Federal Reserve and Treasury provided a total combined $182 billion commitment to stabilize MG, $22.5 billion of which addressed liquidity issues in the securities lending program.

On December 11, 2012, Treasury sold its final shares of MG common stock for additional proceeds of $7.6 billion. Including the proceeds from that sale, the overall positive return on the Federal Reserve and Treasury's combined commitment to stabilize MG during the financial crisis is $22.7 billion. Since 2008, AIG's size as measured by assets has decreased 46 percent and the firm has re-focused on the core business of insurance.

The financial crisis also contributed to the failure of financial guaranty insurers, including both municipal bond and mortgage insurers. *(See* Box 5). Financial guaranty insurers provide protection from credit-related losses on debt products such as municipal bonds, mortgage and other asset-backed securities, and collateralized debt obligations. Bond issuers purchase this insurance, which effectively operates as a guaranty on the bonds, thereby providing better access to the market and reducing borrowing costs. The financial crisis forced several financial guaranty insurers into receivership or run-off. Only one of the firms existing pre-crisis continues to write new business today in the same form as prior to 2008, and that new business is limited to insuring municipal bonds. Exposure to mortgage-backed securities and other structured financial products led to the failure of some of the smaller bond insurers and to credit rating downgrades for the larger insurers, which impaired the ability of those insurers to generate new capital or write new business. These downgrades rippled through the municipal bond markets, causing significant difficulties for both investors and municipalities. State regulators responded by placing some of the financial guaranty insurers into run-off, which refers to a non judicial orderly commercial wind down of the insolvent insurer.

Other parts of the insurance sector were also affected by the crisis. A number of insurers sought and obtained access to federal emergency liquidity assistance, largely to bolster capital for variable annuity products. In addition, state regulators provided direct aid to insurers during the crisis by permitting many insurers to deviate temporarily from NAIC-codified SAP.` *(See* Box 3).

Box 3: Assistance to the Insurance Industry during the Financial Crisis

During the financial crisis, a number of insurers received extraordinary support from governmental entities. This support was provided in the form of: (1) direct capital support by the federal government; (2) liquidity support through credit facilities established by the Federal Reserve; and (3) relief from SAP granted by state regulators.

Direct Capital Support

During the crisis, insurers that were bank or thrift holding companies were eligible to receive capital support from the Capital Purchase Program (CPP) as part of the Troubled Asset Relief Program. Several life insurers acquired regulated thrifts in order to qualify for capital investments available through CPP, although only two received CPP investments. Direct capital support was also provided separately to MG through several complex, multi-step investments from the Treasury and the Federal Reserve.

Liquidity Support

Insurance groups were also beneficiaries of liquidity facilities, primarily from two temporary sources: (1) the Federal Reserve's Commercial Paper Funding Facility (CPFF); and (2) the Term Asset-Backed Auction Loan Facility (TALF) offered by regional Federal Reserve Banks.

The CPFF financed the purchase of unsecured and asset-backed commercial paper from eligible issuers through primary dealers. At the time, significant outflows from the money market sector severely disrupted the ability of commercial paper issuers to roll over short-term liabilities.

The CPFF acted as a liquidity backstop for the commercial paper market. In at least 175 transactions from 2008 through 2009, firms engaged in the business of insurance made use of the CPFF.

The TALF was a credit facility created in December 2007 that allowed a depository institution to bid for a 28-84 day advance from its local Federal Reserve Bank at an interest rate determined by auction. By allowing the Federal Reserve to inject term funds through a broader range of counterparties and against a broader range of collateral than open market operations, TALF provided liquidity when the unsecured interbank markets were under stress.

Non-US. Government Support for Insurers Operating in the United States

In addition to support programs offered in the United States, insurers with substantial U.S. °pent-dons, but domiciled elsewhere, received home-country support. For example, one leading variable annuity writer that generates approximately two-thirds of its income from the United States received approximately $3.7 billion from the Central Bank of its country of domicile.

Another prominent variable annuity writer received more than $13 billion from the Central Bank of its home country and was forced to separate its banking and insurance activities. In addition, several other non-U.S. annuity writers have moved to sell or dispose of U.S. operations due, in part, to the additional capital demands of home country regulators caused by a U.S.-based variable annuity business.

Capital Relief through State Regulatory Permitted and Prescribed Practices

On November 11, 2008, the American Council of Life Insurers (ACLI) requested that state regulators "provide important near term relief from conservative reserve and risk-based capital standards" to help insurers manage the financial stress caused by the financial crisis. The AGLI's proposal and recommendations for expedited change to existing regulatory provisions that governed statutory capital and surplus requirements were rejected by state regulators as a group on January 29, 2009. Nevertheless, throughout the year, state regulators permitted certain insurers to deviate from SAP equivalent to, or in excess of, what was sought by the ACLI. As a result, by allowing revised accounting practices (for example, for deferred tax assets) more favorable than previously allowed by statutory accounting rules and regulations, state regulators provided capital relief to some insurers at a critical time that, in some cases, had a substantial, positive effect on insurer REG ratios.

According to NAIC annual statement data,' 61 life insurance groups reported positive effects on 2008 year-end surplus from state permitted or prescribed practices. The average benefit to surplus among those 61 groups was 9.64 percent. 15 of those groups benefitted by more than $100 million, five of which benefitted by more than $1 billion. 183 P/C insurance groups reported positive effects on 2008 year-end surplus from state permitted or prescribed practices. The average benefit to surplus among those 183 groups was 5.27 percent.

Financial Regulatory Reform

The Dodd-Frank Act introduced reforms to remedy the weaknesses in supervision of the financial system that were exposed through the financial crisis, including those that touched the insurance industry. For example, Title I of the Dodd-Frank Act established a new supervisory structure for the oversight of the U.S. financial system through the creation of the Council, which is charged with identifying and responding to threats to the stability of the U.S. financial system. The Council is authorized to determine that a nonbank financial company shall be supervised by the Federal Reserve and be subject to prudential standards if the Council determines that the nonbank financial company's material financial distress or activities could pose a threat to the financial stability of the United States. The Federal Reserve must establish and enforce prudential standards for the largest bank holding companies and for nonbank financial companies supervised by the Federal Reserve.

The Dodd-Frank Act also addresses insurance more directly by creating HO and by assigning to it an important financial stability role. FIO has the authority and responsibility to monitor all aspects of the insurance industry and to identify issues or regulatory gaps that could threaten the stability of the insurance industry or, more broadly, the U.S. financial system. HO may also recommend to the Council that it designate an insurer as an entity subject to regulation as a nonbank financial company supervised by the Federal Reserve. FIO's financial stability mission also includes playing a role in the context of Title II's Orderly Liquidation Authority. Title II confers "key turning" responsibilities upon HO, whereby the affirmative approval of the FR) Director and two-thirds of the Governors of the Federal Reserve are required before the Secretary may make a determination on whether to seek the appointment of the FDIC as receiver of an insurance company.

Under the FIO Act, FIO's mission also extends to international matters, where FIO is responsible for coordinating federal efforts and developing federal policy on prudential aspects of international insurance matters, including representing the United States, as appropriate, in the IAIS. Until the creation of FIO, a single federal entity had not been specifically designated to represent the United States in discussions about the global insurance regulatory framework and international regulatory standard-setting. FIO's current efforts on prudential aspects of international insurance matters, primarily coordinated through the IAIS, complement the reforms of the Dodd-Frank Act and include: (1) the identification of global systemically important insurers (G-SIIs) to be subject to heightened supervision and regulation; (2) the development of a common framework for the supervision of internationally active groups, including a quantitative capital standard; and (3) the integration of resolution measures into international standards applicable to insurers operating in multiple countries.

III. PRUDENTIAL OVERSIGHT

The Solvency Framework

In the context of insurance, "solvency" generally refers to the ability of the insurer to meet its obligations. Solvency regulation has been and continues to be primarily the responsibility of state regulators. It broadly consists of prudential rules (such as capital requirements and accounting standards, together with guidelines governing investment portfolios), protocols for regulatory intervention with troubled institutions (including insolvency proceedings and requirements for guaranty funds), and supervisory practices intended to promote and maintain the safety and soundness of insurers (including financial examination and analysis, company licensing, and collaboration with regulators from other states and international jurisdictions). Primary financial oversight of any given insurer is performed by the state in which the company is domiciled, *i.e.*, typically where it was formed and maintains its corporate license to operate. Other states generally defer to the regulatory authority of the insurer's domestic state with respect to prudential supervision.[51]

Before the financial crisis, increasing globalization and complexity of the business of insurance had prompted the international regulatory community to reexamine the adequacy of prudential oversight of insurers and the consistency of cross-jurisdictional and cross-sectoral regulatory treatment. The importance of that review has only been underscored by the financial crisis. Currently, domestic and international regulatory discussions around solvency regulation are primarily focused on prudential standards, enterprise risk management, and group (*i.e.*, consolidated) supervision. FIO has authorities that include monitoring all aspects of the industry and the identification of issues or gaps in regulation that could have financial stability consequences, and representing the U.S. government in prudential aspects of international insurance matters. The dual developments of the financial crisis and the unprecedented internationalization of the insurance market have led to increased emphasis on all aspects of solvency oversight, both at the state and federal levels. In addition, international standard-setting activities have grown in importance and focus.

More specifically, the IAIS is the forum through which insurance supervisors and authorities from more than 140 countries, including U.S. state regulators, convene to develop international insurance supervisory standards and best practices. The IAIS does not prescribe a particular approach or structure with which a country must satisfy an international standard.

The Dodd-Frank Act vests FIO with authority to:

> coordinate Federal efforts and develop Federal policy on prudential aspects of international insurance matters, including representing the United States, as appropriate, in the International Association of

> Insurance Supervisors (or a successor entity) and assisting the Secretary in negotiating covered agreements[.][52]

FIO currently represents the United States on the IAIS Executive and Financial Stability Committees, and is involved with the Macro-Prudential Surveillance Subcommittee, along with other subcommittees. FIO's Director also serves as Chair of the IAIS Technical Committee, which leads the development of substantive, technical standards, including the Common Framework for the Supervision of Internationally Active Insurance Groups (ComFrame).

In its role as representative of the United States, FIO consults with state regulators, relevant federal agencies, consumers, insurers, and other stakeholders and technical experts. FIO's current substantive priorities in this capacity are: (1) developing and field testing ComFrame so that it serves supervisors' interests and reflects the realities of insurance industry practices; (2) refining a methodology and process to identify G-SIIs; (3) establishing enhanced supervisory measures to be applied to a G-SII, including cross-border resolution practices; and (4) enhancing insurance group supervision in light of recent Financial Stability Board (FSB) recommendations. While FIO is not a functional regulator, these international prudential matters fall within the ambit of the authority to develop federal policy on prudential aspects of international insurance matters. In addition, FIO's authority to monitor all aspects of the insurance industry, including its regulation, bring these matters of financial stability and the standards applicable to internationally active insurers directly within FIO's area of focus.

On October 16, 2013, the IAIS released a third version of a draft consultation paper that outlines ComFrame. ComFrame is designed to establish a comprehensive framework for supervisors to: (1) address activities and risks at the insurance group level; (2) develop principles for better global supervisory cooperation; and (3) foster global convergence of regulatory and supervisory measures and approaches. The ComFrame concepts, as presently drafted, are likely subject to revision and refinement through the results of the important field testing phase, which is in its early stages and will study the impact of ComFrame's qualitative and quantitative requirements. Through the development of common supervisory approaches, implementation of ComFrame should reduce the compliance and reporting burden on the increasing number of insurers operating in multiple international jurisdictions, and increase the shared confidence of global supervisors. In addition, ComFrame seeks to further understanding of group structures through risk analysis and transparency. Improved consistency of supervisory approaches to solvency oversight would promote more effective and efficient supervision of groups, build trust among the international supervisory community, and foster markets that allow for the participation of U.S.-based insurers.[53]

In 2010, the FSB instructed the IAIS to develop a methodology to identify G-SIIs and the enhanced prudential measures to which designated firms would be subjected. The IAIS established the Financial Stability Committee (FSC), in which FIO has participated since July 2011 and been actively engaged since April 2012. FIO's FSC priorities have been to work with national and international colleagues to ensure the rigor and quality of the IAIS methodology, as well as to align the IAIS process with the Council's three-stage process for determining whether a nonbank financial company should be designated for supervision by the Federal Reserve.

Insurers, in contrast to banks, are not currently subject to uniform capital requirements at the global level. On July 18, 2013, the FSB issued mandates to change that, directing the IAIS to make tangible progress in the following areas:

- As a foundation for Higher Loss Absorbency (HLA) requirements (*i.e.* higher capital requirements) for G-SIIs, the IAIS will develop a Straightforward Backstop Capital Requirement (SBCR) to apply to all group activities, including non-insurance subsidiaries, to be finalized by the end of 2014.
- Building on the SBCR, and following public consultation, the IAIS will, by the end of 2015, develop implementation details for HLA requirements. These will apply starting from January 2019 to those G-SIIs identified in November 2017, using the IAIS methodology.
- The IAIS will develop, and the FSB will review, a work plan to develop a comprehensive, group-wide supervisory and regulatory framework for Internationally Active Insurance Groups (IAIGs), including a quantitative capital standard (QCS). The timeline for the finalization of the framework will be agreed by the FSB by the end of 2013.

On the same day the FSB issued these mandates, it also announced that, in consultation with the IAIS and national authorities, it had identified an initial list of G-SIIs. The population of IAIGs—approximately 50-60 firms from around the world—would include all nine G-SIIs. The IAIS has been considering alternatives for an SBCR. These proposals will be released for a

60- day public consultation beginning in December 2013. Through 2014, the IAIS will finalize an initial version of the SBCR and alternative approaches for the application of HLA requirements to the G-SIIs. Even once finalized, the SBCR will be subject to testing and refinement in the years leading to 2019. Whether the SBCR serves as a basis for HLA, whether the QCS will build on the SBCR, or whether the QCS will serve as the basis for HLA, remain open questions.

The IAIS released a revised draft of the ComFrame concept paper for a 60-day public consultation on October 16, 2013. This version of ComFrame includes a capital adequacy assessment process that would subject an insurance group to a series of plausible and adverse scenarios. At the same time, ComFrame's QCS will be developed in concept by the end of 2016 and, thereafter, will be tested for two years before being finalized in late 2018.

Development of international insurance capital standards remains a daunting and unprecedented challenge. Nevertheless, driven by the fast-paced internationalization of insurance markets, IAIS members appear committed to achieving the stated objectives. Of necessity, the SBCR will be simpler and less granular than the QCS, although development of both will be guided by the boundaries of time, resource and achievability.

Another significant development in solvency oversight has been the EU's 2009 adoption of a regulatory framework known as Solvency II. Solvency II will soon be adopted by the European Parliament as part of an omnibus legislative package, with a scheduled implementation date of 2016. Notably, despite the previous delays with adoption in the EU, components of Solvency II have been adopted in other countries, including China and Mexico.

Broadly structured around the three pillars of capital, supervision, and disclosure, Solvency II would require adherence to RBC requirements at both the individual regulated entity and group levels, whether pursuant to a standardized formula or based on the insurer's own internal models subject to supervisory review. (*See* Box 4). As originally formulated, Solvency II would have been particularly consequential for the U.S. insurance sector because of its requirement for unilateral assessments of insurance regulation in other jurisdictions (including the United States) and because it would impose solvency requirements on insurers doing business in the EU to the extent the home jurisdiction's requirements are deemed to be unsatisfactory in comparison to Solvency II. Through the EU-U.S. Insurance Project (*see* Box 4), the EU and the United States have committed to a collaborative work plan that will enhance understanding and cooperation and, where appropriate, promote greater consistency between the two jurisdictions. Thus, the orientation of the discussion has been altered by virtue of the EU-U.S. Insurance Project which will lead, where appropriate, to the increased convergence and compatibility of the two insurance regulatory regimes.

Finally, in the United States, in December 2012, state regulators released a Solvency Modernization Initiative (SMI) Roadmap, which they describe as a critical self-examination designed to update the states' approach to solvency oversight. Among the areas reviewed are capital requirements, governance and risk management, group supervision, statutory accounting and financial reporting, and reinsurance. The SMI Roadmap also reports state regulators completed adoption of the Risk Management and Own Risk Solvency Assessment (ORSA) Model Act, which comprises enterprise risk management requirements and standards for insurers, together with the *ORSA Guidance Manual*. The SMI Roadmap also notes that state regulators adopted the NAIC Insurance Holding Company System Regulatory Act to provide state regulators with authority, albeit indirect, over non-insurance entities in an insurance group. State regulators also continue to develop task forces and working groups to address, or to discuss, substantive matters such as group supervision, reinsurance captives, and monoline insurers. Most recently, in March 2013, the NAIC released a white paper on the merits of state regulation that reports on the states' efforts to address known challenges for the state-based system.

Box 4: Europe's Insurance Regulatory Regime - Solvency II

Overview of the Three Pillars

In the EU, the European Parliament and European Commission (EC), and the European Insurance and Occupational Pensions Authority (EIOPA) are modernizing the EU's insurance regulatory regime under the Solvency II Framework Directive. The directive, introduced in 2007 and enacted in 2009, will be the culmination of work begun in the early 1990s to update existing solvency standards. Despite a few setbacks and modifications, Solvency II's implementation date now set for 2016.

Solvency II establishes a risk-based approach to insurer capital requirements that relies on three pillars, modeled after the three pillared Basel II framework for banks. The pillars of Solvency II consist of (1) substantive and quantitative RBC requirements; (2) system of governance; and (3) market discipline through disclosures to supervisors and the public.

Pillar I sets target capital levels for a given insurer based upon either a standard formula or subject to regulatory approval, an insurer's internal models. The standard formula is a stressed Value at Risk (VaR) calculation that looks to capture the full set of risks that an insurer faces, including underwriting risk (life, nonlife, health), market risk, counterparty credit risk and operational risk.

Pillar I targets capital requirements for insurers at a level that, based on the VaR analysis, would allow for only a 0.5 percent chance of failure over a one-year time horizon. These capital and related reserve requirements were the subject of an EU impact study, particularly as applied to annuity-like products with long-term guaranty features.

Solvency II would also establish a comprehensive supervisory regime for insurance groups that includes a single group supervisor and consolidated capital requirements for insurance groups. Despite the existence of issues that have delayed full implementation, Solvency II remains the aspirational supervisory regime for the EU. Moreover, many aspects of Solvency II have become international standards for insurance supervisors in developing economies and in mature economies seeking to modernize an existing supervisory regime. For example, capital assessment elements of Solvency II are important elements in the revised supervisory regimes in Mexico, China and South Africa. Furthermore, EIOPA and the World Bank have signed an operational Memorandum of Understanding to cooperate on developing the global insurance sector, which includes promoting a risk-based regulatory and supervisory framework in insurance, as well as the identification of systemic risk and the promotion of consumer protection.

Pillar II, the system of governance, imposes requirements on insurers and groups with regard to risk management and internal control systems, as well as with regard to key functions which, at a minimum, must include the risk management, compliance, audit and actuarial functions. Pillar III sets forth requirements for information to be reported to supervisors and for information to be publicly disclosed so as to enable assessments of an insurer's overall financial condition in addition to market trends and risks.

Regulatory Regime Equivalence

Solvency II includes a provision by which the EC determines whether non-EU regulatory systems provide a similar level of protection to policyholders as would the Solvency II regime, and are therefore "equivalent" to Solvency II.

The equivalence assessment would be based on three criteria, two of which relate to group supervision and one of which relates to reinsurance supervision.

Insurers in "equivalent" jurisdictions would be able to *access* the EU market, and EU based insurers would be able to access non-EU markets, without the imposition of additional capital requirements or restrictions. Insurers in non-equivalent jurisdictions would need to undertake structural changes to "ring-fence" European assets from non-EU assets, including, for example, the creation of separate holding companies within EU jurisdictions.

EU-U.S. Insurance Project

For several years, uncertainty over how the EU "equivalence" assessment would affect U.S. companies had a negative impact on firms operating in the two jurisdictions. To address the issue, in January 2012, 110 hosted representatives of the EC, EIOPA, and state regulators to facilitate a dialogue to improve understanding and cooperation between the EU and U.S. insurance regulatory regimes and, where appropriate, to foster convergence. To this end, the parties developed a work plan for 2012, which consisted of identifying and comparing the significant aspects of each jurisdiction's regulatory scheme. On December 21, 2012, after executing the year's work plan, all parties agreed upon objectives for future work to improve convergence and compatibility. The objectives are to:

1) Promote information sharing between EU and U.S. supervisors under conditions of professional secrecy by removing barriers to the exchange of information while seeking to uphold critical confidentiality standards.

2) Establish a robust regime for group supervision, under which there is:

a) A clear designation of tasks, responsibilities and authority among supervisors, including a single group/lead supervisor;

b) A holistic approach to determining the solvency and financial condition of the group that is consistent with insurance business practices, that avoids double-counting of regulatory capital and that monitors risk concentrations, considers all entities belonging to the group, and is complementary to solo/legal entity supervision;

c) Greater cooperation and coordination among supervisory authorities within colleges; and,

d) Efficient enforcement measures at the group and/or solo level that allow for effective supervision of groups.

3) Further develop an approach to valuation that more accurately reflects the risk profile of companies, is sufficiently sensitive to changes in that risk pmfile, and has capital requirements that are fully risk-based, based on a clear and transparent calibration and that cover similar categories and subcategories of risk to which companies are exposed.

4) Work to achieve a consistent approach within each jurisdiction and examine the further reduction and possible removal of collateral requirements in both jurisdictions in order to ensure a risk-based determination for all reinsurers in relation to credit for reinsurance.

5) Pursue greater coordination in relation to the monitoring of the solvency and financial condition of solo entities and groups through the analysis of supervisory reporting. The exchange of information is facilitated by the joint exchange of best practices for analysis and an evolution towards a greater consistency of reporting.

6) Ensure the consistent application of prudential requirements and commitment to supervisory best practices through different peer review processes that ensure an independent view of the jurisdiction being examined.

7) Ensure consistency and effectiveness in the supervision of solo entities and groups.

Each of the foregoing objectives is supported by a number of initiatives to be pursued over a five-year period. A copy of the "EU-U.S. Dialogue Project Technical Committee Reports Comparing Certain Aspects of the Insurance Supervisory and Regulatory Regimes in the EU and the United States," and of the "EU-U.S. Dialogue Project: The Way Forward," can be found on the HO web site. While marking a significant step towards improving cross-border oversight between the EU and the United States, the Project also facilitates a level of convergence that will benefit industry, consumer, and supervisory interests. In addition, the objectives for each of the seven areas are fundamental to the modernization and improvement of the U.S. system of insurance regulation. Given the national importance of the agreed-upon objectives of this project, failure of the U.S. state regulatory system to pursue adoption of these objectives could warrant greater federal involvement.

Capital Standards

The Current Framework and the Challenge of Non-Uniformity

Recommendations: (1) For material solvency oversight decisions of a discretionary nature, states should develop and implement a process that obligates the appropriate state regulator to first obtain the consent of regulators from other states in which the subject insurer operates; (2) To improve consistency of solvency oversight, states should establish an independent, third-party review mechanism for the National Association of Insurance Commissioners Financial Regulation Standards Accreditation Program.

Insurers, like other financial institutions such as banks, are subject to capital requirements. Capital requirements for insurers, however, are not determined in the same manner as are those for banks. This in part reflects the differences in banks' and insurers' business models, risk profiles and balance sheets. Banks generally lever balance sheets with deposits and debt (some short-term) and use those funds to underwrite loans and to engage in capital markets activities. Assets that banks finance are designed to earn returns from the spread between the interest earned on the long-term assets and the interest paid on short term liabilities. Banks face both credit risk and interest rate risk on those assets and liquidity risk on the ability to fund short-term operations and liabilities. The bank capital regime is therefore designed largely to address credit and liquidity risk, although banks with trading activities also are subject to market risk capital regulation.

Insurers, by contrast, typically do not carry much debt either in unsecured debt at the holding company level or in short-term wholesale funded debt at the entity level. Rather, insurers are primarily funded through investment income and policyholders' premiums, the latter of which are paid periodically and in advance in exchange for insurance coverage that pays out when an insured event occurs. Insurers typically invest premiums received in liquid assets (frequently bonds) that typically match the duration of liabilities. Since insurers typically have less leverage than banks and prefund insurance liabilities by investing premium income, insurers generally are not subject to the kind of liquidity risk that banks face. Insurers are subject primarily to underwriting risk and market risk (including both interest rate risk and credit risk).

State regulation, which directly regulates only insurance entities, requires insurers to satisfy RBC requirements. RBC does not set a capital target for an insurer but, rather, sets a baseline capital level such that, in the event an insurer approaches that baseline level, a state regulator may take corrective action to conserve or improve the insurer's financial condition. RBC requirements are grounded in a basic risk-based methodology that takes four categories of risk into account. Briefly, these risks are: (1) asset risk, which covers market and credit risks on balance sheet assets, including bonds, equities and other financial assets, as well as reinsurance receivables and investments in subsidiaries; (2) insurance risk, which covers risks related to the underwriting and pricing of policies and contracts, as well as risks related to the adequacy of claims reserves; (3) interest rate risk, which covers potential losses due to interest rate changes and asset/liability mismatch; and (4) business risk, which covers guaranty fund assessments and general business risks, such as litigation.

NAIC Financial Regulation Standards Accreditation Program

States have sought to establish generally consistent solvency oversight approaches across jurisdictions through the NAIC Financial Regulation Standards Accreditation Program (Accreditation Program). Following the wave of insurer insolvencies in the 1980s, the Accreditation Program was developed as a response to Congressional inquiries into the regulation of insurers. The Accreditation Program evaluates member states for substantial compliance with NAIC-established solvency oversight standards and practices. Accreditation standards are minimum standards against which states are assessed on not more than a five year cycle.

To be accredited, a state must have in force laws that are substantially similar to the significant elements that have been identified as the key provisions in each of the relevant NAIC model laws or regulations. If a state fails to meet the accreditation standards and loses its accreditation, then the work of that state regulator in maintaining and enforcing insurer solvency standards for its domestic industry will not receive deference from other states' regulators. Although several states have been subjected to tentative accreditation pending improvement, no state has ever lost its accreditation. All states are now accredited, with the State of New York having been accredited most recently in 2009.

Notwithstanding the foregoing efforts to establish consistency in capital regulation, significant elements of non-uniformity remain. First, for example, even though RBC standards have been adopted by all states, those standards are not applied to all insurers.

Some states allow certain classes of insurers not to comply with RBC requirements. For example, fraternal benefit societies operating as life insurers are treated differently for RBC purposes and only 14 states have adopted the applicable model law.

Second, as another example, monoline insurers (*e.g.*, mortgage insurers and financial guaranty insurers) are not subject to RBC requirements; instead, these entities have been subject to different capital ratio requirements that are enforced differently from state-to-state. Up to and through the crisis, state regulators granted waivers from adherence to capital ratio requirements in order to allow mortgage insurers to continue operating. These developments are particularly noteworthy given the subsequent history of insolvency with much of the financial guaranty business and the challenges encountered by mortgage insurers, including insolvency. (*See* Box 5).

Box 5: Credit Rating Agencies, Financial Guaranty Insurance, and the Financial Crisis

Credit rating agencies (CRAB) have played a twofold role in the insurance industry: (1) providing views of an insurer's solvency to policyholders and lenders; and (2) rating financial instruments in an insurer's investment portfolio. Both roles significantly inform the amount of capital that insurers hold. Some state that the role of CRAB in assessing the targeted capital levels that insurers and groups should hold based on risk profiles is as or more important than that of the state regulators which, through RBC, focuses on a quantifiable basis on the amount of capital necessary for individual insurers (but not groups) to avoid regulatory intervention.

The financial crisis highlighted pervasive problems with the CRA business model and practices, such as conflicts of interest, inadequate controls, and unreliable ratings methodologies. The ratings assigned by CRAB on many assets turned out to be higher than warranted. Belated downgrades of assets caused significant market disruption.

One example of CRAB' failure was the incorrect assessment of the health of financial guaranty insurers. Financial guaranty insurers are organized as "monoline" insurers because state insurance regulations generally prohibit these firms from writing other types of insurance. The financial crisis showed that the monoline nature of the business, together with the performance of the assets underlying the guaranties, contributed to insolvencies of financial guaranty insurers.

For many years, the assets guaranteed by most financial guaranty insurers, such as mortgages and municipal bonds, were generally considered low-risk because of historically low default rates. As a result, financial guarantors held low levels of capital with the consent of the regulators. On the same rationale, financial guarantors received top ratings from CRAB notwithstanding low capital levels and the eventual movement from the core business model to provide guaranties on assets such as riskier structured products, including collateralized debt obligations consisting of mortgage-backed securities.

During the crisis, as the number of defaults on the underlying assets increased, the mortgage-backed securities were downgraded and dropped in value. Financial guaranty insurers were forced to recognize losses which eroded already thin layers of capital. The loss recognition in turn caused CRAB to downgrade these insurers, thereby subjecting the insurers to a vicious cycle of collateral calls and additional market pressure, which further accelerated loss recognition. The losses for financial guaranty insurers contributed to temporary dislocation in the municipal bond market, and limited the access of municipal issuers to the market. Since the crisis, much of the municipal bond market has moved forward without the wrap of a financial guaranty. The Dodd-Frank Act requires the Securities and Exchange Commission (SEC) to adopt rules to govern CRAB on conflicts of interest, ratings performance and methodology transparency, strengthening internal controls policies and procedures, improving governance, and training and competency standards for credit analysts. In addition, Section 939A of the Dodd-Frank Act requires federal agencies to remove regulatory references to credit ratings and to replace those references with alternative measures of creditworthiness and reliance.

State regulators have sought to decrease the influence of credit ratings both by expanding the role of the NAIC's Securities Valuation Office (SVO) and by retaining contractors to evaluate the quality of collateral underlying mortgage-backed securities. The SVO, which has historically provided credit ratings for insurers and supervisors for non-rated securities, now also offers high level guidance and insights for both insurers and supervisors. With respect to mortgage-backed securities, the NAIC engaged contractors, at industry expense, to support the move away from rigid dependence on credit ratings. These contractors are responsible for reviewing the loss probabilities in mortgage-backed securities based on the underlying collateral and aiding in the determination of the NAIC designations that translate into RBC factors.

Third, RBC standards are not necessarily applied uniformly. The lack of uniformity occurs largely because of a range of discretionary decisions by state regulators that can affect the reported or actual amount of an insurer's capital. These discretionary decisions can occur in a number of areas, but some of the more important decisions that affect solvency oversight involve decisions regarding reinsurance captives and permitting deviations from standard accounting practices. Although supervisory discretion may be necessary for some regulatory purposes, a principal concern with extensive and inconsistent use of such discretion is that it may effectively exempt an insurer from abiding by capital requirements, thereby undermining the comparability of the RBC framework across different jurisdictions. Such variability has the potential to create safety and soundness concerns. Moreover, such inconsistent discretionary decisions create competitive imbalances that disadvantage insurers domiciled in one state solely because that regulator's discretion may be more circumspect than that of the lead state regulator of a competitor.

It is important for accounting and capital standards, and discretionary variances from those standards, to be governed by uniform rules. Under the current system of state regulation, consistency can occur only by uniform adoption and implementation of such standards and rules. As noted, however, the regulatory system has not resulted in consistent implementation of solvency oversight, notwithstanding coordination efforts through the NAIC, because regulators have interpreted and enforced even similar standards differently.

Two reforms could assist the coordination efforts and further improve uniformity and consistency. First, variations resulting from discretionary practices can be reduced if state regulators develop and implement a process whereby before implementing a discretionary practice involving important solvency oversight matters, the domestic state regulator notifies and also obtains the consent of regulators from other states in which the subject insurer operates. In the case of insurers operating in multiple states, such an approach would require, at a minimum, the concurrence of insurance regulators from multiple states prior to permitted deviation from significant solvency standards. For insurance groups that are subject to supervisory college oversight, consent of other regulators could be obtained through the ongoing activities of the college.

Second, the credibility and effectiveness of the Accreditation Program could be bolstered if it becomes also subject to independent, third party review. Currently, only state regulators, NAIC staff, and NAIC contractors are charged with evaluating states' compliance with the Accreditation Program. States often consult with the NAIC's legal staff when considering adoption of model laws and regulations, yet it is the NAIC's legal staff that is solely responsible for assessing compliance of states with adoption of the key elements of model laws and regulations. To improve the reliability of this peer review structure, an additional independent review and audit layer would provide a helpful perspective on the uniform adoption and implementation of capital rules and other standards. This independent review will also help to maintain the incentive for accreditation reviews to be conducted with appropriate and objective rigor.

Mortgage Insurance

Recommendation: Federal standards and oversight for mortgage insurers should be developed and implemented.

Like financial guarantors, private mortgage insurers are monoline companies that experienced devastating losses during the financial crisis. A business predominantly focused on providing credit enhancement to mortgages guaranteed by the government-sponsored enterprises (GSEs), Fannie Mae and Freddie Mac, mortgage insurers migrated from the core business of insuring conventional, well-underwritten mortgage loans to providing insurance on pools of Alt-A and subprime mortgages in the years leading up to the financial crisis. The dramatic decline in housing prices and the impact of the change in underwriting practices required mortgage insurers to draw down capital and reserves to pay claims resulting in the failure of three out of the eight mortgage insurers in the United States. Historically high levels of claim denials, including policy rescissions, helped put taxpayers at risk.

Regulatory oversight of mortgage insurance varies state by state. Though mortgage insurance coverage is provided nationally, only 16 states impose specific requirements on private mortgage insurers. Of these requirements, two govern the solvency regime and, therefore, are of particular significance: (1) a limit on total liability, net of reinsurance, for all policies of 25 times the sum of capital, surplus, and contingency reserves, (known as a 25:1 risk-to-capital ratio); and (2) a requirement of annual contributions to a contingency reserve equal to 50 percent of the mortgage insurer's earned premium. In addition to the states, the GSEs (and through conservatorship, the Federal Housing Finance Agency) establish uniform standards and eligibility requirements that in some cases are more stringent than those required by state regulators. As the financial crisis unfolded, mortgage insurers no longer met state or contractual capital requirements. State regulators granted waivers in order to allow mortgage insurers to continue to write new business while the GSEs loosened other standards that were applicable to mortgage insurers.

The private mortgage insurance sector is interconnected with other aspects of the federal housing finance system and, therefore, is an issue of significant national interest. As the United States continues to recover from the financial crisis and works to reform aspects of the housing finance system, private mortgage insurance may be an important component of any reform package as an alternative way to place private capital in front of any government or taxpayer risk. Robust national solvency and business practice standards, with uniform implementation, for mortgage insurers would help foster greater confidence in the solvency and performance of housing finance. To achieve this objective, it is necessary to establish federal oversight of federally developed standards applicable to mortgage insurance.

Captives and the Impact on Capital in the Life Insurance Industry

Recommendation: States should develop a uniform and transparent solvency oversight regime for the transfer of risk to reinsurance captives.

Captive insurance programs, in the conventional meaning, typically are entities (usually corporate affiliates set up by a parent company) that provide a self-funded insurance-like product for a single non-insurance business. Captives include a diverse set of entities and are most often established to meet the unique needs of the owner. For example, a large manufacturing firm may establish a captive to cover property damage to its facilities around the country.

However, captives also have developed as a tool for insurers to transfer risk within the affiliated insurance group. A reinsurance captive, sometimes referred to as a special purpose vehicle, or SPV, allows an insurer to transfer risk to an affiliated entity, thereby reducing reserve obligations and freeing the underlying insurer's capital to be used for other purposes. However, reinsurance captives are not subject to the same solvency oversight as a traditional commercial insurer or reinsurer. Thus, reinsurance captive programs can be mechanisms by which insurers decrease capital and reserves at the insurance-entity level through intra-group reinsurance arrangements while also reducing overall regulatory scrutiny across the group.

Over the past 30 years, the use of captives has grown from less than 1,000 captives in 1980 to over 5,000 operating worldwide today.[54] In particular, U.S. commercial life insurers' use of reinsurance captives to transfer insurance risk has grown, perhaps due to reserve requirements for some life insurance and annuity products. In the United States, almost 30 states, the District of

Columbia and the U.S. Virgin Islands serve as domiciles for reinsurance captives.[55] Indeed, states are aggressively competing to be domestic regulators for reinsurance captives.

There are two basic concerns with reinsurance captives that are increasingly prevalent in the life insurance business. The first is that reinsurance captives allow an insurer to receive credit against its reserve and capital requirements by transferring risk to the captive even though the captive is not bound by rigorous or consistent capital rules across the states. Reinsurance captives can be established with a small percentage of the capital required to establish a commercial insurance license in the same state. In particular, the standards that govern the quality of capital that reinsurance captives must hold are not sufficiently robust. For example, some state laws currently allow intra-company letters of credit, parental guaranties, or intra-company guaranties to constitute capital for captives. These instruments may not be sufficiently loss-absorbing if a significant adverse event were to occur. In many cases, a significant adverse event would cause a captive to fail and spread losses retained within the holding company or to another affiliate within the group, thereby accentuating group risk.

If an insurer is to receive credit against a capital or reserve requirement because of risk transferred to an insurance captive, the rules governing the quality and quantum of assets offered in support of the captive should be uniform across states and sufficiently robust and transparent in order to prevent arbitrage by insurers. The matter is one that must be assessed within the rubric of the capital adequacy of an insurance group as a whole. Under the current state-based capital adequacy regime, group capital assessments rely on CRA ratings or on a firm-produced ORSA to evaluate a group's capital position and the strength of intra-group guarantees. Neither of these measures of group capital adequacy, however, is a substitute for group capital standards that are established and supervised by regulators.

Second, there is a lack of transparency for captive oversight from state-to-state. While transparency to investors and the public is important, transparency to regulators is particularly critical and absent. Unlike the case of traditional insurers for which financial statements are made publicly available on the NAIC's website or the websites of the domestic state and the company itself, the financial statements of captives are kept confidential between the captive manager and the domestic state. Due to the limits of state regulatory authority, this concern is especially critical when a state regulator must rely on information from another state in which a reinsurance captive is domiciled.

In response to these issues and to the increased use of reinsurance captives, the NAIC commenced a review of state approaches to captives in October 2011. The NAIC received comments on a draft white paper on regulation of reinsurance captives, released on November 29, 2012, which offered five recommendations addressing accounting, confidentiality and reinsurance regulatory matters. The NAIC then issued a revision of the white paper on June 6, 2013. While this paper showed the regulator dialogue was continuing, it notes the lack of agreement among the states on issues of transparency and confidentiality, on whether captives should be assigned a company code and name and included in the regulators' company database, and on how to address inconsistencies between the current approach to reinsurance captives and the more general laws governing credit for reinsurance (where the reinsurer is a third party company, as opposed to an affiliate within the same group). The comments illustrate that several states seek greater regulatory scrutiny and uniformity in captive oversight, while others remain committed to the status quo. Still other states are interested in reducing oversight fees and premium taxes for reinsurance captives, possibly to allow jurisdictions to attract more reinsurance captive enterprises for economic development purposes.

On June 12, 2013, the New York Department of Financial Services (NYDFS) issued a report that details the initial findings of an investigation into the use of reinsurance captives by life insurance companies as a capital arbitrage vehicle. The NYDFS found that New York-based insurers and affiliates alone accounted for $48 billion of "shadow insurance" capital manipulation. The NYDFS report found that existing state-based disclosure regulations are inadequate, inconsistent, and incomplete to properly identify and regulate these transactions; and that reserves were diverted and risk-based capital was artificially boosted, misleading regulators, investors, and the general public. The NYDFS report identified regulatory inadequacies in transparency with respect to the use of letters of credit, parental guarantees, and other forms of capital permitted by state captive regulators but not disclosed or made publicly available.

To modernize and improve state-based oversight of reinsurance captives, states should develop and adopt a uniform and robust standard for transparency, not only of the liabilities transferred to a reinsurance captive, but also of the nature of the assets that support a reinsurance captive's financial status. As part of such an oversight regime, states should develop and adopt a uniform capital requirement for reinsurance captives, including a prohibition on those types of transactions that do not constitute a legitimate transfer of risk, e.g. that do not provide the protections intended by the Credit for Reinsurance Model Law. Subject to limitations on the disclosure of legitimately proprietary information, these transactions should be disclosed in the financial statements of the ceding insurer. Finally, states should develop and adopt nationally-consistent standards for oversight of the reinsurance captive industry that includes public disclosure of the financial statements of such captives, adopting nationally-consistent standards for oversight of all captives, and adopt those standards as a feature of the Accreditation Program.

Issues Surrounding RBC Methodology and Adequacy Determination

Recommendation: State-based solvency oversight and capital adequacy regimes should converge toward best practices and uniform standards.

The RBC framework has been criticized both on the basis that it is too prescriptive and rigid and that it is too permissive and fails to adequately capture economic and other risks. For example, one stated shortcoming is that RBC applies a single framework to all insurers regardless of size, complexity, and risk profile. Other criticisms of the RBC methodology are that it relies on static statutory accounting valuation of assets and liabilities instead of economic valuations, that it uses pre-determined factor-based calculations instead of dynamic risk models, and that the risk weights for certain assets and liabilities should be modified (e.g., those for investment assets and reinsurance recoverables[56]). The criticisms also state that the current RBC methodology lacks explicit quantification for key risks, that certain risks are currently not captured in RBC at all (such as catastrophe and operational risks, the so-called "missing risks" issue), and that the risks are calibrated in a manner that is not clear or consistent. State regulators are reviewing the RBC framework and intend to address certain of the foregoing criticisms of the methodology, including the "missing risks" issue and adjustment of certain risk weights.

To complement RBC requirements, state regulators have also begun to develop a risk assessment regime whereby insurers make annual self-assessments of capital adequacy and report those annual determinations to state regulators. The self-assessments, known as ORSA, would include stress testing and a requirement to detail risk management systems and policies. If adopted by the states as presently contemplated, the self-assessment obligations would apply both to a statutory insurance entity and to a consolidated group engaged in the business of insurance. For firms operating in the United States and also the EU, consideration should be given to the convergence of EU and state-based ORSA requirements in order to minimize redundant or duplicative reporting requirements for participating insurers.

As state regulators work to refine the RBC methodology and develop ORSA, two important considerations should be kept in mind. First, programs such as ORSA present the question of whether state regulators possess sufficient resources with the prerequisite technical skills and experience to review the complex insurer self-assessments of risk and capital adequacy. If ORSA requires significant investments in actuarial modeling expertise and professional services, state regulators may confront significant challenges to meet those needs. If state regulators move to reliance on third-party contractors for an ORSA assessment, a uniform national standard should be used to determine qualified contractors, as well as a means to assure that state regulators adequately understand, and are accountable for, the work and findings of such contracted specialists.

Second, solvency oversight and capital adequacy principles should be attuned to international developments and should endeavor to integrate best practices, standards and principles that are developed through international consensus. As major participants in the business of insurance become increasingly global in operation, it is important for insurance regulatory authorities to guard against capital arbitrage across international jurisdictions.

Reserving

For insurance purposes, reserves are liabilities that are reported on insurers' balance sheets for the ultimate payment of future losses and policyholder benefits. Reserves are often set using factors and rates determined by an insurer's actuary consistent with guidelines established in state law for insurance products. Reserve levels for insurers operating in the United States and offering certain life insurance and annuity products have been set according to a state law rules-based formula that, insurers claim, results in excessive reserves that detract from the insurer's ability to maximize the value of its capital. For example, in the life insurance sector, insurers complain that reserve requirements for certain products fail to reflect current mortality rates and fail to integrate the insurer's particular business mix and risk profile.

Principles-Based Reserving

Recommendation: States should move forward cautiously with the implementation of principles-based reserving and condition it upon: (1) the establishment of consistent, binding guidelines to govern regulatory

practices that determine whether a domestic insurer complies with accounting and solvency requirements; and (2) attracting and retaining supervisory resources and developing uniform guidelines to monitor supervisory review of principles-based reserving.

As required by state law or regulation, life insurers currently calculate reserves for life insurance policies based on a standardized formula prescribed by the Model Standard Valuation Law (SVL) of the NAIC. Although the SVL's prescribed valuation mortality table is based on U.S. population data and contains a prudent margin for reserving, the reserve calculated is not specifically tailored to the circumstances of any insurer because it does not consider more particular attributes of policyholders in individual insurer portfolios. Critics of the current formula-based approach to reserving for life insurance contend that it: (1) is static and too conservative; (2) fails to capture all the particularized risks inherent in increasingly complicated life insurance benefits and guaranties; and (3) does not reflect life insurers' business practices, such as the hedging of risk through derivatives use plans. However, reserves are subjected to an annual asset adequacy test analysis to verify the adequacy of reserves through different stochastic and deterministic models, with additional reserves established if necessary. Many industry participants argue that redundant reserve requirements force reliance upon reinsurance captives in order to reduce excessive reserves and allow life insurers to efficiently use capital.

For nearly a decade, state regulators have been considering a move to principles-based reserving (PBR) to address these concerns. Whereas the formula-based approach to quantifying reserves uses standardized calculations, PBR relies upon an insurer's internal risk modeling and analysis techniques, including the use of insurer-specific claims experience with specific portfolios of business, to incorporate consideration of particularized risks and thereby to more closely tailor calculations to the actual attributes of insurer portfolios. State regulators adopted a supporting Valuation Manual (Manual) at a December 2012 NAIC meeting that contains details of the principles-based approach and defines the methods for calculating life insurer reserves. However, legislative adoption of the revised SVL by a supermajority of states (42) representing at least 75 percent of the nationwide premium volume is needed along with a supermajority NAIC adoption of the Manual before the Manual and PBR become operative.

The difficulty with consistent adoption, interpretation and enforcement of a principles-based approach under the current system of insurance legislation and regulation was evident through the Valuation of Life Insurance Policies

Model Regulation (Regulation XXX), which establishes reserve requirements for life insurance products with secondary guarantees, and Actuarial Guideline 38 (AG 38). AG 38 was first adopted by the NAIC in 2003 to address questions pertaining to Regulation XXX such as clarifying reserve requirements for new universal life insurance product designs. AG 38 was revised in 2005 to clarify guidance applicable to sophisticated shadow fund designs and in 2007 to provide an interim solution for reserving for universal life with secondary guarantees with respect to certain matters. Notwithstanding these revisions and clarifications, different state regulators had different interpretations regarding the meaning of AG 38, resulting in competing firms holding more (or less) capital in reserve, depending on the jurisdiction. This state-by-state variance led to competitive imbalances and substantial criticism from industry participants and observers. State regulators have pursued a solution whereby reserving for prospective policies is premised on an agreement negotiated between several states and the life insurance industry, but the agreement does not address marketplace imbalances that result from previously divergent state regulator interpretations. As even this example of a successful compromise demonstrates, full consistency among states is difficult to achieve.

The U.S. life insurance sector's reserving requirements should properly reflect current mortality rates, the life insurer's business model, and its particular risk profile, but substantial concerns arise with the prospect of a wholesale adoption of PBR. In addition to consistency issues, state regulators will also face the challenge of maintaining a sufficiently high level of expertise for understanding the "black box" of the models on which reserve levels would be established. Specifically, the need for many more sufficiently trained and expert actuaries and examiners than are currently available to regulators raises necessary questions with respect to the states' ability to verify insurers' implementation of PBR in a uniform manner that is consistent with the Manual. Furthermore, the state-by-state interpretation and application of PBR means consistency across the states will be difficult to achieve. To obtain necessary expertise, states likely would have to contract with consulting actuaries and other professionals, many of whom may have clients in the life insurance industry and, thus, state regulators will need to sort through and manage potential conflicts of interest.

Following the leadership of New York, state regulators in California, Florida and North Dakota, among others, established a working group through the NAIC to recognize the challenges of implementing PBR but allowing the implementation to move forward. Recently, however, the NYDFS identified flaws and raised serious questions about the efficiency of the working group process. Some industry leaders oppose the effort as an initiative that could lead to further weakening of the state solvency oversight regime.

States should move forward with substantial caution to implement PBR. State regulators require significant additional technical expertise or resources to properly evaluate the rigor and quality of idiosyncratic reserve models that vary among firms within a heterogeneous insurance industry. Therefore, states should also adopt standards for the oversight of the vendors who will provide related consulting services to the states.

Credit for Reinsurance

Recommendation: To afford nationally uniform treatment of reinsurers, FIO recommends that Treasury and the United States Trade Representative (USTR) pursue a covered agreement for reinsurance collateral requirements based on the National Association of Insurance Commissioners Credit for Reinsurance Model Law and Regulation.

Reinsurance is a risk management mechanism whereby insurers transfer, or "cede," risk to an "assuming" reinsurer. The state-based capital regime for insurers recognizes the value of reinsurance typically by permitting the insurer to reduce its reserve liabilities in some proportion to the risk that is ceded to a reinsurer. This also can reduce the insurer's capital requirements as determined by RBC.

Under the current state regulatory regime, states insurance regulators do not have direct oversight over non-U.S. reinsurers, but instead regulate the solvency of those U.S. insurers that purchase reinsurance. If a reinsurer is based in the United States, then the ceding carrier receives 100 percent credit on its financial statement to the extent that gross liabilities are transferred, or ceded, to that reinsurer. In most states, however, if the reinsurer is a non-U.S. firm, and if it is not licensed, accredited, or approved by the regulator of the state in which it seeks to provide reinsurance, the reinsurer typically must post qualifying collateral equal to 100 percent of the actuarially estimated reinsurance liabilities that it has assumed from the ceding insurer in order for the ceding insurer to receive full credit. This is true even though non-U.S. reinsurers typically are not required to have a domestic license in order to write business in the United States, and regardless of the financial strength of the foreign reinsurer or the strength of the supervisory regime in the reinsurer's home jurisdiction. The issue is particularly significant because non-

U.S. reinsurers play a large role in the U.S. market, accounting for at least 58 percent of the reinsurance premium volume that is ceded by U.S.-based insurers.[57]

This collateral requirement has long been a subject of discussion within the domestic and international reinsurance sector. Proponents of collateral requirements often refer to the importance of reinsurance recoverables to the U.S. insurance marketplace. Others point to the solvency impact on the primary insurer in the absence of adequate collateral if reinsurance fails to deliver according to a contractual promise. Critics of the current system, on the other hand, maintain that a determination of whether a reinsurer should post collateral should be more sensitive to evolving risk-based considerations. Other related questions in this discussion have been the basis and extent to which regulators should recognize the capital regimes in reinsurers' home jurisdictions, the impact of collateral requirements on reinsurance capacity, and the increased costs for insurers and consumers.

In November 2011, state regulators, working through the NAIC, unanimously adopted amendments to the Credit for Reinsurance Model Law and Regulation (Model Collateral Law) that, if enacted at the state level, would authorize the state regulator to certify unauthorized reinsurers for reduced collateral regulatory standards. As of July 2013, the NAIC reports that 18 states have adopted some form of authorization for the state regulator to accept less than 100 percent collateral from non-U.S. reinsurers, but the authorization is not uniform in structure or implementation. Among other requirements of the Model Collateral Law, for an unauthorized reinsurer to be certified, the reinsurer must be domiciled and licensed in a jurisdiction deemed to be "qualified." The determination of whether a non-U.S. jurisdiction is qualified would be made by each state regulator, based on the quality of regulation in the non-U.S. jurisdiction, among other criteria. If a state regulator concludes that a non-U.S. jurisdiction is qualified, the Model Collateral Law, if applied, would then require the state to make a further determination as to the quality of the reinsurer. The state is to assign a "secure level" rating based, at least in part, on the opinion of a CRA. This rating would then be used to determine the minimum level of collateral required by the reinsurer for the ceding insurer to receive 100 percent credit against capital requirements for the reinsurance.

Recent state regulator action on this topic has been noteworthy and constructive. The Model Collateral Law represents a step forward but it remains incomplete. For example, a determination by one state within the United States of the adequacy or the equivalence of regulation by another nation would not bind other states. One consequence might be that a foreign jurisdiction could link insurance determinations by a state to other economic or regulatory issues pending between the United States and the affected foreign jurisdiction, possibly frustrating broader U.S. economic or regulatory policy.[58] The Model Collateral Law also has other features that require further deliberation. For example, it depends too heavily upon assessments of reinsurers' creditworthiness by CRAs. It would be preferable for other, more risk-based empirical factors to be the basis upon which to determine creditworthiness. Sound credit risk management practices by ceding insurers, and not reliance on CRAs or regulatory measures, should be the basis on which collateral relief is provided.

Under Title V of the Dodd-Frank Act, FIO and the United States Trade Representative (USTR) are authorized, jointly, to negotiate and enter into "covered agreements." Specifically, such "covered agreements" would relate to the recognition of prudential measures with respect to the business of insurance or reinsurance that achieve a level of protection for insurance or reinsurance consumers that is substantially equivalent to the level of protection achieved under State insurance or reinsurance regulation. Such agreements may be necessary to impose uniformity on a prudential insurance matter of national interest.[59] As part of such an analysis, FIO would consider pending prudential regulatory issues affecting the United States and relevant foreign jurisdictions.

FIO is authorized to coordinate federal efforts and develop federal policy on prudential aspects of international insurance matters. In formulating federal policy, FIO is well-positioned to make determinations regarding whether a foreign jurisdiction has sufficiently effective regulation and, in doing so, would consider other economic or regulatory issues pending in the United States and between the United States and affected foreign jurisdictions.

State regulators have worked constructively to move forward with enactment and implementation of the Model Collateral Law. Given the likelihood that the Model Collateral Law would be of non-uniform application, together with the complicating effect of state-by-state inconsistency on economic matters of national interest, the circumstances warrant the pursuit of covered agreements for reinsurance collateral requirements. Indeed, the Model Collateral Law could form the basis for such covered agreements. To afford nationally uniform treatment of reinsurers, FIO recommends that Treasury and USTR pursue a covered agreement for reinsurance collateral requirements based on the NAIC Credit for Reinsurance Model Law and Regulation.

Corporate Governance – Director and Officer Suitability and Fitness

Recommendation: States should develop corporate governance principles that impose character and fitness expectations on directors and officers appropriate to the size and complexity of the insurer.

Corporate governance is a broad and expanding area of supervisory interest, particularly for those firms based or operating in the United States that also have international operations. Accordingly, state regulators do have a practice of checking the fitness of insurer management and directors, as they consider the background of officers in determining whether that person is suitable to act as an insurance executive or key owner. When an insurer is initially formed, for purposes of issuing a license to operate, state regulators evaluate the character and fitness of prospective owners, directors or officers by evaluating the individual's biographical information. In some instances, this review is limited to determining whether the individual has a history of criminal wrongdoing. After an insurance entity is operating, state regulators review changes on the board of directors and officers with oversight that is often limited to an evaluation of whether the individual self-reports a prior conviction for criminal behavior. State regulators allow an individual to serve in an insurer's leadership position upon receiving notice, but may later revoke that tacit approval if the individual is proven to be unqualified or a threat to policyholders.

Even though state regulators conduct fitness reviews, there is an absence of state law or regulation applicable to corporate governance specific to insurers. In 2012, the NAIC compiled a summary of existing corporate governance requirements for U.S.-based insurers. With regard to insurance regulation, the NAIC summary described various governance-related aspects of prudential oversight requirements for: (1) an insurer's financial reporting and audit functions; (2) the monitoring of an insurer off- and on-site and through examinations and ongoing analysis; (3) solvency oversight; (4) regulatory authority over transactions; (5) authority of regulators to take corrective action in respect of a troubled insurer; (6) the authority of state regulators to operate a receivership; and (7) other processes such as authority over market conduct examinations and rate regulation. The summary also described non-insurance related governance standards, including from the Securities Act of 1933 and the Sarbanes-Oxley Act of 2002.

The absence of an NAIC Model law or regulation governing insurer corporate governance has also been noted by international authorities. The

International Monetary Fund (IMF) conducts a Financial Sector Assessment Program (FSAP) to help countries identify and remedy weaknesses in their financial sector structures, thereby enhancing resilience to macroeconomic shocks and cross-border contagion. FSAP assessments are designed to assess the stability of the financial system as a whole and not that of individual institutions. For the insurance sector, supervisory practices are measured against the IAIS Insurance Core Principles. In 2009-2010, the IMF conducted an FSAP of the United States financial system, including state regulatory oversight of the insurance sector. In its review, the IMF concluded there are "no NAIC model laws or regulations that address corporate governance directly."

Notwithstanding the absence of authoritative rules and guidelines, insurers have increasingly focused on governance and risk management matters since the financial crisis. In recent years, for example, many insurers have elevated the prominence of a chief risk officer within the corporate hierarchy. In addition to increased focus by insurers, regulatory authorities and standard-setting bodies have been engaged in sustained work on corporate governance issues.

The focus on corporate governance should continue and become more defined. Many U.S.-based insurers are expanding rapidly in geography, size and complexity, thereby imposing even greater demands on leadership. For example, internationally active insurers are increasingly engaged in sophisticated enterprise risk management practices to measure and understand risks posed to the enterprise from any angle or perspective. With standards appropriately scaled to the size and complexity of the firm, state regulators should adopt director and officer qualification standards that require individuals serving in those roles to have the expertise to assess strategies for growth and risks to the enterprise. For an insurer that exceeds size and complexity thresholds, state regulators should adopt an approach designed to ensure that individuals nominated to serve in the firm's leadership ranks have sufficient capacity to understand and challenge an insurer's enterprise risk management.

Group Supervision

Recommendation: (1) In the absence of direct federal authority over an insurance group holding company, states should continue to develop approaches to group supervision and address the shortcomings of solo entity

supervision; (2) state regulators should build toward effective group supervision by continued attention to supervisory colleges; and (3) FIO should engage in supervisory colleges to monitor financial stability and identify issues or gaps in the regulation of large national and internationally active insurers.

State regulators are authorized to supervise insurers at the individual entity level, but lack the legal authority to supervise a non-insurance affiliate or any affiliate domiciled and operating outside of the state. These inherent limitations of state law constrain any particular state regulator from conducting oversight over or obtaining information regarding the operations of a multi-jurisdictional insurance group such as a large, complex global insurance firm.

The absence of state regulatory authority over non-mutual holding companies (i.e., solo entity supervision) and the existence of only indirect authority over non-insurance entities within an insurance group raise concerns with respect to regulatory acceptance of U.S. insurance firms that desire to engage in the business of insurance outside of the United States. International supervisors from other developed and emerging economies – markets in which U.S.-based firms are seeking to expand – continue to evaluate the relative strengths and weaknesses of solo entity supervision, particularly with respect to solvency matters. To date, actions taken against U.S.-based firms to remedy shortcomings of state-based solo entity supervision have been few, but that may change in the coming years. For example, non-U.S. supervisors may determine that solo entity supervision is inadequate for large, complex financial firms, especially when those firms have significant market share; if so, then the foreign supervisors may take unilateral remedial action against those firms.

Experience with recent insurer insolvencies, moreover, illustrates that a comprehensive understanding of an insurance group could have resulted in a safer and more stable system. Since 2000, the largest U.S. insurer insolvencies were attributable to a variety of causes, but the important facts in common among these cases indicate that a group regulator armed with comprehensive supervision of the enterprise may have prevented those failures or resulted in earlier action that could have stemmed the losses. One firm failed due to mismanagement and fraud, including the shifting of assets between affiliates and the holding company that could more easily have been detected absent the diffusion of state regulatory responsibility. Another firm failed due to inadequate rate-setting which, if subjected to appropriate enterprise risk management oversight, could have exposed deficient pricing, inadequate reserves and the inadequacy of support by the holding company for its licensed entities. A consolidated group supervisor with knowledge of an insurer's enterprise risk management and intra-company transactions, together with the appropriate authority, could have been in a position to improve the supervision of the failed firms to help assure the safety and soundness of those firms.

The limits on state regulatory authority hamper effective regulation at a time when insurers are increasingly part of internationally active, diversified financial conglomerates that engage in a variety of non-insurance businesses. The inability of this regulatory structure to account for consolidated supervision was evident during the financial crisis, particularly in the case of AIG. The Dodd-Frank Act partly addresses this shortcoming of the state regulatory system by introducing provisions on consolidated supervision of the financial activities of nonbank financial companies supervised by the Federal Reserve, as determined by the Council. However, the insurance regulatory system itself should be reformed to provide for group supervision.

State regulators have taken steps to improve solo entity supervision and to make such entities less vulnerable to the weaknesses of affiliates or the group. For example, the regulations of many states require prior approval of certain investment and reinsurance transactions between insurers and non-insurer affiliates, and generally require prior approval by the state regulator before capital can be removed from an insurer.

State regulators may also have the indirect authority to seek information concerning a non-insurer parent or affiliate. Specifically, through the NAIC, state regulators adopted a revised Model Insurance Holding Company System Regulatory Act and Regulation in 2010 (Holding Company Model Act), which grants the state regulators only indirect authority over non-insurance affiliates and the holding company. However, given that direct state regulatory authority is limited to the state-licensed legal entity, there are substantial questions as to how effective the Model Insurance Holding Company System Regulatory Act and Regulation can be and whether the law's indirect authority actually grants insurance regulators effective authority over non-insurance affiliates or holding companies. The NAIC has reported that the revised Holding Company Model Act has been adopted in 14 states and is pending in 15 others. The actual statutory language and implementation has varied among those states in which the Holding Company Model Act has been adopted.

In addition to the Holding Company Model Act, state regulators, working through the NAIC, are evaluating enhancement of group supervision as part of the SMI process. The principal proposal in SMI adopts a "windows and walls" approach that would "provid[e] a window into group operations, while building upon, rather than rejecting, the existing walls which provide solvency protection," to insurers. The proposal identifies the following "regulatory windows": (1) the coordination of state participation on a national level for sharing information with international regulators; (2) supervisory colleges for internationally active groups; and (3) access to information about unregulated entities within the holding company system.

The NAIC is considering additional guidance in its Financial Analysis Handbook to address group-wide supervision. The proposed changes cover topics such as the scope of group supervision, coordination and cooperation with supervisors in other jurisdictions, holding company and group-wide financial analysis, a financial examination assessment, roles and responsibilities of the group-wide supervisor/ lead state, corporate governance, enterprise risk management, and the supervisory college.

The state of group supervision in the United States has drawn international attention. In its 2010 FSAP, for example, the IMF stated with respect to insurance group supervision: "The U.S. approach is focused on securing the financial soundness of individual insurance companies. While this has not been unusual among insurance regulators internationally, many have been supplementing their strong solo company focus with financial and other requirements and more supervisory focus applied at the group level and U.S. supervisors should do the same. They do not currently make an assessment of the financial condition of the whole group of which a licensed insurance company is a member."[60]

In the absence of direct federal regulation of insurance groups, supervisory colleges will be an important means of addressing the conduct of group supervision in the intermediate term. The IMF similarly recommended that the United States further develop group supervision and establish international supervisory colleges to supervise U.S.-based insurance groups with international operations.

A supervisory college should be a forum that includes all of an insurance group's functional regulators, both domestic and international, to meet and to share information relating to the supervised group, and identify trends or areas of strength or weakness within the group. A supervisory college should also establish a system in support of group supervision and offer a formal mechanism for increasing regulatory communication and collaboration. For example, the IAIS ComFrame project will significantly improve the operation, efficiency, and substantive value of supervisory colleges for both supervisors and insurance groups. States have undertaken good faith efforts to establish and operate supervisory colleges, and many are in the nascent stages of development.

Supervisory colleges established for U.S. firms operating nationally and internationally, and for nonU.S. firms with large operations in the United States, should also include FIO in light of FIO's statutory mission to monitor all aspects of the insurance industry, including issues or gaps in regulation, and FIO's significant role with respect to financial stability. The financial stability perspective brought by FIO would be important for the functioning of the supervisory colleges and, similarly, the information made available to FIO through activity in the supervisory college would be highly significant to FIO's explicit statutory role as financial stability monitor for the insurance industry.

Supervisory colleges are necessary but not sufficient, and do not completely substitute for a consolidated regulator. For example, members of a supervisory college may find it difficult to reach consensus on important issues and the processes by which the college decides or acts may prove to be inefficient. Given concerns about the adequacy of solo entity supervision for larger groups, particularly for U.S.- based firms operating globally, consolidated supervision for large, internationally-active U.S.-based insurance firms will require continued focus and national attention.

Resolution of Insolvent Insurers

The resolution of insolvent insurance entities is governed by state receivership law, specifically the law of the insurance entity's state of domicile. Recent developments stemming from the financial crisis, however, have prompted re-evaluation of the extant resolution regime for insurance entities. While there already have been reforms with respect to the resolution of large, internationally active insurers, further reforms of the resolution regime should be considered.

Resolution of Large, Internationally Active Firms

Establishing an authority that would implement an orderly resolution of a failed financial firm is an essential component of the Dodd-Frank Act. In the case of insurance firms, the Dodd-Frank Act provides that orderly resolution under Title II will take place under prevailing state law. In addition, before the Secretary may make a determination on whether to seek the appointment of the FDIC as receiver of an insurer under Title II, the Secretary must first receive a written recommendation from the FIO Director and the vote of two-thirds of the Governors of the Federal Reserve then serving.

Although resolution of a licensed insurance entity largely occurs under state law, a number of factors suggest that it would be important for resolution planning for complex, global insurance firms to involve analysis and preparedness extending beyond the framework of state-based receiverships and guaranty funds. Consideration of resolution plans for complex U.S.-based national and international insurance firms indicate, for example, that: (1) non-insurance subsidiaries, affiliates and holding companies do not participate in guaranty funds or state-based receiverships; (2) insurance entities may sell products excluded in whole or in part from guaranty fund protection; and (3) insurance entities are not always included in the guaranty fund scheme. These realities mean that, in some cases, a significant part of the activities of an insurance group will fall outside of the states' resolution scheme for insurers. In these cases, separate, holistic orderly resolution plans should be developed for globally active insurers.

Resolution of insurers is a focus of the international regulatory agenda. In that regard, in 2013, the FSB stated that it will focus on three main objectives: (1) addressing the remaining obstacles to implementation of resolution strategies such as cross-border cooperation and information sharing among supervisors; (2) launching an effective assessment process to evaluate the resolvability of all global systemically important financial institutions, including G-SIIs; and (3) developing guidance for the resolution of insurance and other nonbank financial institutions.[61] With respect to insurance in particular, the FSB will initiate a thematic peer review on resolution regimes. This will include a cross-jurisdictional review of the adequacy and effectiveness of resolution regimes for nonbank institutions, including insurers, particularly if the failure of those firms could raise financial stability concerns. The FSB is working with the IAIS to develop further guidance on the features and powers necessary for resolution regimes to meet FSB standards.

Receivership

Recommendation: States should: (1) adopt a uniform approach to address the closing out and netting of qualified contracts with counterparties; and (2) develop requirements for transparent financial reporting regarding the administration of a receivership estate.

Insurer resolution proceedings typically begin with the filing of a petition by a state attorney general, acting on the recommendation of the regulator of the insurer's domicile. If the petition is granted, the state regulator will be appointed receiver. Once the insurer is in receivership, the state regulator generally has three options: conservation; rehabilitation; or liquidation. In a conservation, the state regulator attempts to preserve the status quo while additional information is gathered to determine whether a more assertive approach in receivership (i.e., rehabilitation or liquidation) is needed. In a court-supervised rehabilitation, the state regulator submits to the court a plan to restore the insurer to a solvent capital position. If a feasible rehabilitation plan cannot be developed, or is proposed but not approved by the court, or if the plan proves unsuccessful, a state regulator will then seek a court order allowing for liquidation that will lead to distribution of any insurer assets to policyholders and claimants in accordance with state law.

The determination as to whether and, if so, when to place an insurer into conservation, rehabilitation, or liquidation is subject to the discretion of the domestic state regulator. State political, consumer, and economic development issues may impact the timing of state regulator action. Furthermore, permitted accounting practices can subvert the intent of other solvency tools, such as RBC. The NAIC created the Financial Analysis Working Group (FAWG) to provide a forum of peers to engage with domestic state supervisors of a troubled insurer. FAWG is often cited by the NAIC as an effective means to help states consider appropriate courses of action. Nonetheless, any course of action is entirely dependent upon the authority, discretion, and will of the domestic state regulator.

Following the solvency crisis in the 1960s, states adopted resolution laws and receivership protocols in certain important areas. For example, state laws generally protect policyholders and claimants in a receivership proceeding by elevating those claims to priority over other creditors. Policyholder and claimant protection sometimes takes the form of ring-fencing some assets of an insurer's receivership estate and prohibiting the use of those funds to pay other estate liabilities. An example of such ring-fencing, which has widespread adoption among the states, is protecting owners of variable annuities backed by "separate accounts," which hold assets that are largely segregated from the insurer's general assets and liabilities.

Beyond issues surrounding policyholder and claimant protection, however, insurer resolution laws vary both in specific terms and in application across different states. There have been efforts to impose greater uniformity on state receivership laws. In 1978, state regulators developed the first model law on insurer resolution. To date, however, only 32 states have adopted this template in whole or in part. In 2005, the NAIC published the Insurer

Receivership Model Act but, to date, only two states have enacted legislation based on this model law.

One important area in which there are state-by-state differences is the treatment of derivatives and other qualified financial contracts (QFCs) once an insurer is in receivership. The federal bankruptcy code provides protections to counterparties on QFCs by exempting these transactions from the automatic stay and allowing counterparties to terminate and close out QFCs on a net basis. While the Federal Deposit Insurance Act (FDI Act)[62] and foreign bankruptcy laws also provide similar protections to QFC counterparties, only some state resolution laws do. The lack of inclusion of uniform close-out netting and other protections for QFCs in state insurance receivership laws has potential negative consequences for insurers and for the financial system. For example, an insurer operating in a state with resolution laws that do not include QFC protections may find it difficult and far more costly to participate in derivatives markets. In addition, the absence of these QFC protections in many state laws could have negative implications for financial stability since these provisions are designed in part to reduce interconnectedness between firms. Accordingly, states should adopt a uniform approach to address the closing out and netting of QFCs with counterparties.

The status and cost of a receivership estate are issues in which policyholders and other creditors have a keen interest, but too often there is a lack of sufficient, clear, and timely information. In 2008, the NAIC announced the release of its Global Receivership Information Database (GRID) which serves as a publicly accessible repository of information about open and closed estates being administered by state insurance regulators (or their designees) as receiver. GRID includes administrative elements such as contact information for the receiver, court order references, lines of business that had been written by state, and distributions. The database also provides an opportunity for the receiver to post a financial statement for the estate. The NAIC reported as of March 31, 2013 that there are wide variances among the states as to the extent of information that has actually been made available through GRID, with the data submitted by many states as being less than 25 percent complete. Furthermore, the nature, form, extent, and timeliness of financial information about insolvent insurers and pertinent disclosures by receivers are inconsistent, if available at all. Receivers use various bases of accounting (e.g., cash basis, modified cash basis), with widely varying degrees of detail as to disclosures accompanying the financial statements. States should develop requirements for transparent financial reporting by receivers about the insolvent estate as well as the costs of administration that have been incurred, require timely preparation and filing of reports on a regular basis, and make pertinent aspects of this information publicly available.

Guaranty Funds

Recommendation: States should adopt and implement uniform policyholder recovery rules so that policyholders, irrespective of where they reside, receive the same maximum benefits from guaranty funds.

One condition for operating an insurer in a state is the insurer's participation in the state guaranty fund. State guaranty funds provide for the timely honoring of policyholder claims asserted against an insolvent insurer.

Guaranty funds are administered by state guaranty associations, which are created by state law typically as nonprofit entities and are subject to the oversight and direction of insurers licensed in the state. Most states have established separate funds for different lines of insurance, e.g., separate funds for P/C and for L/H coverage.[63] Guaranty associations dedicated to each line of business participate in national associations – the National Conference of Insurance Guaranty Funds (NCIGF) and the National Organization of Life & Health Insurance Guaranty Associations (NOLHGA).

In the event of an insurer's insolvency, guaranty associations may take a range of steps to offer continuing protection to policyholders. For example, in the typical insolvency of a P/C insurer, state guaranty associations step in to pay the portion of claims within the limits guaranteed by the respective state association. In a L/H insolvency, state guaranty associations may arrange continuing insurance coverage for the failed insurer's policyholders; that can involve entering into "assumption reinsurance" agreements with healthy insurers, whereby the healthy insurer assumes policy liabilities in return for a transfer of the failed insurer's assets. NOLHGA may often assist the various state L/H guaranty associations in the negotiation process and in the transfer of liabilities arising from multi-state L/H insurer insolvencies to a solvent carrier. Guaranty associations may also assume liabilities until such liabilities run off, although this path is less frequently taken.

NCIGF reported that, through 2011, its member guaranty funds have paid more than $26.4 billion to claimants since 1976. NOLHGA states that its members have protected consumers in roughly 75 multistate insolvency cases involving life and health insurers. NOHLGA reports that a significant life insurer has not failed since the early 1990s.[64] However, despite significant apparent capacity in the guaranty fund system, it is unclear how the system would fare in the event of a failure of a large insurance group in the United States. Furthermore, an event that would cause such a scenario would likely impact other insurers as well. Just as insurers perform stress tests under adverse scenarios, NCIGF and NOLGHA should periodically model the potential adverse impacts of such scenarios on the guaranty fund system for review by FIO.

While guaranty funds address many of the consumer protection deficiencies that were experienced during the solvency crises that occurred in the 1960s, 1980s, and 1990s, some important consumer protection considerations remain. For example, laws concerning product pay-outs by guaranty funds to policyholders are not uniform across states. For claims against P/C insurers, maximum payouts per claim are generally set by statute between $100,000 and $500,000, with most state laws imposing a $300,000 cap. For claims against life and health insurers, guaranty funds provide at least $100,000 in coverage for health claims, $300,000 for life claims, $100,000 for cash surrender/withdrawal values, and $100,000 for annuity claims. Although these figures define the general range of protection, there are significant variations among states on these figures. For example, an annuitant in New Jersey is eligible for up to $500,000 of guaranty fund protection, but an annuitant in Indiana with the same product is eligible for up to $100,000 in guaranty fund protection. Consumers who purchase the same coverage or product from the same company may receive a different guaranty fund benefit if they reside in different states at the time the insurer is placed into receivership.

States should enact uniform policyholder recovery rules so that all policyholders, irrespective of where they reside, receive the same benefits from guaranty funds. In the event that states fail to achieve uniformity with respect to guaranty fund benefits, then federal involvement may be necessary to ensure fair treatment of all policyholders.

IV. Marketplace Oversight, Consumer Protection and Access to Insurance

"Marketplace oversight" refers to those aspects of insurance regulation that concern consumer protection, insurance access, and affordability. Marketplace regulation displays substantial state-by-state variance. This variance was the subject of substantial attention in the decade before the financial crisis and prompted a number of members of Congress to introduce legislation to introduce greater uniformity. Insurers and consumer advocates have criticized this lack of uniformity and the absence of coordination on regulatory matters on grounds of duplication, inefficiency, delay, and uneven consumer protections.

This section reviews the areas that are most frequently the subject of discussion in the area of marketplace regulation: producer licensing; approval of insurance products for sale; market conduct examinations; and collection of tax for multi-state surplus lines. This section also addresses issues of affordability and access to insurance, including rate regulation, risk classification, natural catastrophes, and accessibility of insurance for Native Americans.

Producer Licensing

Recommendation: The National Association of Registered Agents and Brokers Reform Act of 2013 should be adopted and its implementation monitored by FIO.

A "producer" is an agent or broker who markets, distributes or sells an insurance product to a consumer. Today, even though an increasing percentage of consumers purchase insurance on-line or through other direct means, insurance products reach the consumer principally through producers. The number of total licensed producers reflects their importance: in 2012, NIPR, an electronic, centralized producer database, reported that nearly 2.3 million individuals maintained more than 6 million state insurance producer licenses.

Producers may not market, distribute or sell insurance in a given state without a license from that state. States have an application process that typically requires providing personal information, completing required education and training, satisfying a background check, and passing a licensing examination. Regulating producers is an important activity for states. Producers often are the principal insurance point of contact for consumers and, therefore, regulating producers' qualifications directly bears on consumer protection. Producer licensing also generates revenue for the states and state insurance departments.

Although approximately 70 percent of producers maintain a license in only one state, the remaining are licensed in two or more states. The differences in licensing requirements among the states can present duplicative obligations and barriers to entering business in a particular state.

There have been steps to promote greater uniformity in licensing practices and requirements. In 1996, the NAIC, with support from the producer community, developed NIPR, which thereafter established the electronic database through which states may obtain and share information about any current or prospective licensee. NIPR now offers a range of services to aid with licensing, including single and multi-state licenses, single and multi-state renewals, and continuing education verification.

A few years later, in 1999, Congress, in enacting GLBA, set a deadline of November 2002 to require that a majority of the states and territories enact uniform producer licensure laws or adopt reciprocity laws. Under GLBA, failure of the states and territories to meet the producer licensing target would have triggered formation of NARAB, an entity to provide multi-state producer licenses. In response to GLBA, however, state regulators developed the Producer Licensing Model Act (PLMA), which sought to create a framework for reciprocal recognition of producers seeking to be licensed in more than one state. In 2002, the NAIC certified that 38 states and territories adhered to the PLMA, thereby complying with GLBA and avoiding creation of NARAB. As of 2009, the NAIC certified that 47 states and territories were in compliance with the PLMA. After the PLMA, state regulators adopted Uniform Licensing Standards, which provide substantive standards for licensing, renewals, and continuing education requirements.

Notwithstanding these efforts, the inconsistencies and inefficiencies resulting from the absence of uniformity in state producer licensing persist. One fundamental reason is the lack of full participation by the states in the reciprocity and uniformity efforts. For example, many states do not offer the full range of services that NIPR makes available. Moreover, NIPR offers services to help with insurer appointments, or with resident licensing and renewal, but these services are not used by many states. In addition, although the NAIC certified that 47 states and territories had adopted PLMA, three that had not were New York, Florida, and California, which are among the largest of the state insurance markets.

Consumers are detrimentally affected by the absence of uniformity and reciprocity in producer licensing. For example, in an increasingly mobile society, many consumers who move across state lines may prefer to maintain a relationship with a producer based in another state. The National Association of Insurance and Financial Advisors reported, however, that 80 percent of its surveyed members were unable to serve a client who moved to another state, and 12 percent of its members were unable to serve 50 or more clients who had moved to a state in which the producer was unlicensed.

The lack of uniformity creates duplicative administrative and regulatory burdens with no corresponding consumer benefit. Small firms (or "agencies") seeking producer licenses in multiple states confront significant resource demands. The Independent Insurance Agents and Brokers of America report that more than 1.6 million producers are licensed in more than one state, requiring time and expense to obtain licenses that could otherwise be used to develop and grow the producer's business portfolio. The resource burden is also felt at large firms. The Council of Insurance Agents and Brokers described one large firm that holds 76,100 licenses nationally for approximately 5,000 licensed individuals, 3,100 of whom are licensed in more than one state. Other firms face similar burdens.

Even adherence to the PLMA does not necessarily result in the needed uniformity. For those states that have adopted the PLMA, reciprocity has not necessarily followed. A business entity that employs individuals who sell, solicit, or negotiate insurance is considered a producer under the PLMA. The reality remains, however, that every state requires these business entities to be licensed producers, which is in addition to the requirement that every individual producer employed by the entity be individually licensed. Some states impose different requirements for the licensing of business entities, including entity appointment requirements, licensing for branch locations, affiliation requirements, and filing of organizational documents. Regardless of the reasons for these differences, each increases the compliance burden without commensurate benefits of consumer protection.

The lack of uniformity persisting in this area, even following explicit Congressional direction through GLBA, warrants Congressional action to establish uniformity and to reduce the burdens of multi-state producer licensing. NARAB II, which has passed the House and is pending in the Senate, would establish NARAB, a corporation solely intended to establish uniformity and efficiency in producer licensing requirements.

Producers licensed through NARAB would be able to conduct business in multiple states, but would not be subject to licensing requirements in every state in which they do business. Rather, they would be licensed through NARAB with the opportunity to conduct business in all the states. Enforcement of state laws applicable to producers would remain with the state regulator.

If NARAB II is passed by Congress, the focus should shift to successful implementation of the legislation. In particular, the interests of consumers, although not directly represented on the proposed NARAB II governing board, should receive due consideration and remain a priority. Further, the NAIC should develop an appropriate mechanism to integrate the concerns of those states whose regulators, as a matter of state law, are unable to serve on the governing board. Finally, NARAB II must provide producers an efficient and streamlined multistate licensing mechanism. Consistent with its authority to monitor all aspects of the insurance industry, if NARAB H is passed by Congress and signed by the President, then HO will monitor the establishment and implementation of NARAB II to ensure that these priorities are achieved.

Box 6: Marriage and Insurance

Recommendation: States should assess whether or in what manner marital status is an appropriate underwriting or rating consideration.

Insurers often use marital status as an underwriting and rating factor. Auto insurers and homeowners' insurers often offer a lower premium for the same coverage to married individuals than to a single person. The use of marital status as an underwriting and rating factor may disadvantage an individual who is lawfully married under the laws of another state to a person of the same sex.

Recent years have seen a number of legal and policy developments at the federal and state levels regarding the treatment of same-sex spouses. To note one example, in *United States v. Windsor'* the Supreme Court recently ruled a provision of the Defense of Marriage Act (DOMA) unconstitutional. That provision provided a federal definition of "marriage" and "spouse" to be used in reference to federal laws and regulations, defining marriage as a legal union between one man and one woman, and spouse as referring only to a person of the opposite sex who is a husband or a wife. The Supreme Court found that that provision "violates basic due process and equal protection principles applicable to the Federal Government" under the Constitution's Fifth Amendment.' Following *Windsor,* federal agencies have reviewed and revised regulations and policies to extend federal benefits and obligations of marriage to same-sex married couples, in a manner consistent with law. For example, the Internal Revenue Service allows a same sex couple lawfully married in one state to be treated as married for tax purposes regardless of whether the laws of the state of residence allow for same sex marriage. In addition, at the state level, Illinois recently became the sixteenth state to allow for same-sex civil marriage.

In light of the recent legal and policy developments in the treatment of same-sex spouses, and based on equality considerations and other factors, states should assess whether or in what manner marital status is an appropriate insurance underwriting or rating consideration.

Product Approval

Recommendation: State-based insurance product approval processes should be improved by securing the participation of every state in the Interstate Insurance Product Regulation Commission (IIPRC) and by expanding the products subject to approval by the IIPRC. State regulators should pursue the development of nationally standardized forms and terms, or an interstate compact, to father streamline and improve the regulation of commercial lines.

State regulators use product approval, or "form regulation," to assess whether insurance products comply with state consumer protection laws, such as those governing insurance policy or contract design, pricing, and coverage terms. The process for product review and approval varies by state, as do the standards with which the insurer must comply. For example, some states require approval before a product is offered in the market, but others permit introduction to the market without prior approval, while still other states reserve the option for later review. The duration of review and substantive standards for review also vary, depending on factors ranging from regulatory processes to state resource constraints.

The absence of a uniform national standard and protocol for product approval is a continuing complaint for insurers that argue the lack of uniformity creates inefficiencies and compromises the ability to offer the same products simultaneously and in the same manner on a nationwide basis. Insurers assert further that both speed-to-market and innovation are harmed by product approval delays in many jurisdictions.

Consumer advocates note that the lack of uniformity creates opportunities for regulatory arbitrage, both with respect to personal and commercial lines insurance.

Box 7: Personal Auto Policies for Service Members

Recommendation: HO will convene and work with federal agencies, state regulators, and other interested parties to develop personal auto insurance policies for U.S. military personnel enforceable across state lines.

Product approval requirements also can disproportionately impact members of the armed forces. Active duty members of the military may transfer to a different base in the United States every 24 to 36 months, which typically involves the member of the armed forces moving to a different state. An individual on active duty can transfer credit cards, checking accounts, and other financial services simply by submitting a change of address form. By contrast, an individual moving from one state to another may be required to obtain a new auto insurance policy on each transfer.

While state laws differ, FIO will work with federal agencies, state regulators, and other interested parties to identify a more accommodating approach for service members who have personal auto policies and are required to move across state lines. For example, a common form for personal lines auto coverage for active duty members of the military could be developed and adopted so that the member's transfer to a new base located in another state does not necessitate a new policy form issuance.

Over the years, states have moved to address some of the shortcomings of the product approval process through thc IIPRC and SERFF. In July 2003, the NAIC adopted the current IIPRC model law. Upon the adoption of the model in a state, the state is allowed to join the IIPRC. The IIPRC develops uniform product standards and improves speed-to-market and uniformity for life insurance, annuity, disability income, and long-term care products. Through the IIPRC, an insurer may submit a life, annuity, disability income, or long-term care product filing to be reviewed and approved by a single reviewing body operating under unitary standards. If a product is filed for approval with IIPRC, its uniform standards supersede those of any compacting state unless the insurer submits that product directly to the compacting state outside of the IIPRC framework. The IIPRC was brought into existence in May 2006 upon meeting the threshold requirement of 26 states or 40 percent of premium volume nationwide. The IIPRC currently has 43 members (42 states and Puerto Rico). None of the compact members have opted out of the uniform standards for life only or annuities products; five members have opted out of the uniform standards for long-term care; six members do not permit Modified Rate Schedule filings for long-term care; and one member has opted out of the uniform standards for individual disability products. In 2012, 167 companies registered to file products for approval and submitted 744 filings, resulting in the approval of 625 products. The average approval time for the products was 23 days.

Notwithstanding the strides represented by the formation and function of the IIPRC, for several reasons uniformity and efficiency have yet to be achieved in the area of product approval for life insurance, annuities, long-term care, and disability products. First, state participation in IIPRC is incomplete, largely because California, Florida, and New York have not joined, and the populations of those states constitute a substantial portion of the U.S. insurance market. Second, the scope of product lines eligible for IIPRC review is limited, and the IIPRC has yet to develop approval standards for group annuity, group long-term care or group disability products. Finally, IIPRC permits an insurer to submit an approval request directly to a state IIPRC member, thereby allowing an insurer to circumvent IIPRC standards completely. Accordingly, insurers have the ability to avoid the IIPRC consumer protection standards if those standards are more stringent than the consumer protection standards of the state IIPRC member, thus making IIPRC a regulatory tool susceptible to arbitrage.

Given the shortcomings, dissatisfaction among life insurers persists. In 2011, ACLI's survey of its members found that 83 percent believe that improvement of policy/contract form approval processes is of "critical/major importance." Life insurers assert that the lack of uniformity in a rapidly evolving and growing market for retirement products stifles product innovation.

States should take the following measures in the short term. First, non-participating states should join the IIPRC. For states with a constitutional or legal impediment to joining a multi-state compact, state regulators should adopt the IIPRC product standards and processes as model law and regulation. Second, such standards should serve as a baseline so as to allow states with higher consumer protection standards to continue enforcing those higher standards. Third, to remove opportunities for arbitrage, state regulators from member states should prohibit insurers from opting into less restrictive non-IIPRC standards. Finally, IIPRC should expand the scope of its product coverage and develop standards for all products within its authority.

In 1998, state regulators established SERFF to standardize initial product filings with the regulators and to expedite submitting insurance policy forms for approval. With SERFF, insurers can simultaneously file for product approval in multiple states but the legal and regulatory standards for form review remain different state by state.

Regulatory approval of policies sold to sophisticated commercial policyholders, though presently subject to less regulatory scrutiny than policies for individuals and families, often impose substantial delay and may have the unintended consequence of driving more commercial policyholders to less regulated surplus lines coverage or self-insurance. In a 1998 NAIC white paper entitled *White Paper on Regulatory Re-engineering of Commercial Lines Insurance: Streamlining of Commercial Lines Insurance Regulation,* state regulators recommended, among other things, a flexible regulatory stance for form and rate review in markets found to be competitive by the state regulator, exemptions for large commercial policyholders from form and rate review, and authority for state regulators to waive specific policy requirements for policyholders primarily located in another state. In the 15 years since that white paper the states have made important strides.

Nonetheless, commercial lines insurance regulation must continue to modernize. Inconsistent and sometimes lengthy product approval periods continue to limit the ability of insurers to meet the needs of national businesses with new products. Although most states permit exemptions for large commercial policyholders from rate or form review, the premium volume or number of employees that qualify an insured as a large commercial policyholder vary by state. Additionally, while the creation of SERFF has achieved efficiency gains, insurers continue to identify inconsistencies in SERFF filing requirements by state that limit those efficiencies for multistate filings.

Recently, the NAIC formed the Commercial Lines (EX) Working Group to ascertain the extent to which states moved forward with the recommendations included in the 1998 white paper as well as to consider additional reforms in the commercial lines market. As part of this work, state regulators should pursue the development of nationally standardized forms and terms, or some mechanism for interstate reciprocity, to streamline and improve the regulation of commercial lines.

Given the importance of efficiency and consistency in the product approval process for many insurance products, FIO should continue to monitor state-based product approval processes. Federal action may become necessary if the current, and long-standing, shortcomings are not improved in the near term.

Box 8: Sale of Annuities to Suitable Consumers

Recommendation: In order to fairly protect consumers in all parts of the United States, every state should adopt and enforce the National Association of Insurance Commissioners Suitability in Annuities Ransactions Model Regulation.

One of the most important financial decisions facing many consumers approaching retirement is whether to invest their savings by purchasing annuities, shares in mutual funds, or interests in other securities. Financial literacy among consumers varies widely and it is difficult for many consumers to evaluate what investments are most suitable. Whether an annuity is suitable for a particular consumer and what specific contract features best meet the consumer's needs depends upon a variety of considerations, including the consumer's age, income, financial situation, and risk tolerance. In addition to state regulation, federal law, including the Employee Retirement Income Security Act, may govern the provision of investment advice concerning annuities.

All annuities offer the advantage of the deferral of tax on the investment earnings, with the earnings taxed as ordinary income only when the annuitant actually receives the annuity payment. There are three general types of annuities. Fixed annuities pay a pre-determined flat monthly sum. Variable annuities pay a monthly sum determined by the performance of an investment portfolio held in a segregated account. Indexed annuities have a guaranteed minimum payment with the opportunity for a higher payment depending on the performance of another asset or underlying rate or index, such as a selected securities index.[67] Each of these types of annuities can be paid for a specific period of time or for the life of the annuitant.

State regulators supervise the sale of all commercial annuity products, and licensed insurance producers may sell annuities. In addition, variable annuity products are also considered securities and are regulated by the SEC.[68] Consequently, licensed insurance producers selling variable annuities must be appropriately affiliated with a member of the Financial Industry Regulatory Authority (FINRA) and comply with registration requirements applicable to a sec ti fides representative.

Through the NAIC, following numerous state enforcement actions, state insurance commissioners have attempted to create a national suitability standard for annuity sales. The NAIC Suitability in Annuity Transactions Model Regulation (Model Suitability Regulation) requires:

(1) insurance producers to have reasonable grounds for believing that the recommendation to buy an annuity- is suitable for the consumer; (2) insurers to maintain procedures for review of each recommendation to purchase an annuity to determine suitability prior to issuing the annuity; (3) insurance producers to be trained on the provisions of annuities generally; and (4) a safe-harbor for variable annuity sales made in compliance with FINRA requirements.[69]

The Dodd-Frank Act provides incentives for state regulators to enact national suitability standards. The Dodd-Frank Act authorizes the Office of Financial Literacy in the Consumer Financial Protection Bureau (CFPB) to issue grants to states to enhance the protection of seniors from misleading and fraudulent sales of financial products."' State regulators could, for example, apply for the grant if, among other requirements that may be established by the CFPB, the state regulator were to adopt suitability standards that meet or exceed the Model Suitability Regulation. The Dodd-Frank Act also directs the SEC to treat indexed annuities as exempt securities if: (1) the value of the indexed annuity does not vary according to the performance of a separate account; (2) the indexed annuity satisfies state nonforfeiture law or in the absence of such, the NAIC Model Standard Nonforfeiture Law for Life Insurance or NAIC Model Standard Nonforfeiture Law for Individual Deferred Annuities; and (3) the indexed annuity is issued in a state that has adopted the Model Suitability Regulation or by an insurer that adopts and implements practices on a nationwide basis for the sale of annuity contracts that meet or exceed the NAIC Model Suitability Regulation.[71]

The United States has entered an era of unprecedented levels of retirement age residents. Financial security for the aging population is an essential priority, and that security must be shaped around the unique circumstances of each retiree.

The suitability of an annuity purchase should not be dependent upon the state in which the consumer resides. Given the importance of national suitability standards for consumers considering or purchasing annuities, states should adopt the Model Suitability Regulation. In the event that national uniformity is not achieved in the near term, federal action may become necessary.

Market Conduct Regulation

Recommendation: States should reform market conduct examination and oversight practices and: (1) require state regulators to perform market conduct examinations consistent with the National Association of Insurance Commissioners Market Regulation Handbook; (2) seek information from other regulators before issuing a request to an insurer; (3) develop standards and protocols for contract market conduct examiners; and (4) develop a list of approved contract examiners based on objective qualification standards.

Regulators formally review an insurer's compliance with state laws governing market conduct practices through market conduct regulation. Market conduct regulation includes market analysis, investigations and market conduct examinations. Investigations or market conduct examinations may be commenced either as part of a regular schedule or on an ad hoc basis, when the regulator becomes aware of circumstances that raise market behavior concerns, whether through the receipt of information from customer complaints, other supervisors, other insurers, the media, or other sources. Currently, investigations and market conduct examinations may be conducted by the regulator of any state in which an insurer operates and may cover any matter within that state's laws, including licensing, underwriting practices, claims settlement, use of forms, and customer service.

Market conduct regulation has been the focus of significant criticism by industry and third-party commentators. The principal reasons are that state regulators often fail to adequately coordinate market conduct examinations, resulting in multiple examinations for the same or similar sets of issues, with all the attendant burdens and inefficiency. A 2003 Government Accountability Office (GAO) report[72] noted that states not only differed in the rigor and breadth of market conduct examinations – thus raising concerns also about effective consumer protection – but that coordination between states was inconsistent and infrequent.

In response to these shortcomings, state regulators have taken steps to create a more systematic, structured and uniform market conduct regulation program. Although a Market Conduct Surveillance Model Law, adopted by state regulators at the NAIC in 2004, has not been widely adopted, the NAIC Market Regulation Handbook (Handbook), has been adopted by most jurisdictions, and describes the key components and standards for: (1) market analysis; (2) investigations; and (3) market conduct examinations. Aside from adopting common examination protocols, state regulators collaborate and coordinate market conduct regulation through the NAIC Market Actions

Working Group (MAWG). This forum permits states to share information gained through market analysis, investigations, or market conduct examinations. Based on this information, a state regulator may proceed with a multi-state market conduct examination.[73]

Notwithstanding these improvements, when the GAO revisited the market conduct examination process in 2009, it determined that states had improved the process, but that differences among the states still limited progress toward appropriate coordination and standardization of examinations. The GAO acknowledged that states had developed some market conduct guidance, data collection, and analysis tools, but noted that substantial variances continued among the states in terms of process, criteria, and coordination. Indeed, as of 2011, 45 of 56 NAIC jurisdictions required insurers to submit a Market Conduct Annual Statement (MCAS), a compilation of insurer-specific market conduct-related data. However, a 2011 ACLI survey of its members noted continued dissatisfaction with market conduct regulation. The ACLI survey noted that 63 percent of respondents rated current market conduct practices as "unsatisfactory/needs improvement," with 78 percent citing a lack of uniformity as the major cause of dissatisfaction, along with "speed/timing," "cost," and "expertise/capacity."

State regulators have continued to work on improvements to market conduct regulation and conducted a self-survey to understand current state activities.[74] A 2012 NAIC survey demonstrates the continued variation in market conduct regulation among the states: one state carried out 66 percent of all interrogatories conducted in 2010, three states carried out 48 percent of all specialized data calls, and one state accounted for 73 percent of all reviews of insurers' self-audits. The survey asked whether states would be willing to forgo an examination of an insurer if another state had conducted an examination and ensured all of the issues of concern were corrected. Respondents noted this would depend on the comparability of the state's market conduct examination system, whether the insurer was a domestic insurer, the severity of the issues, and the similarity of state laws.

Coordination between states and standardization of market analysis, investigations and examinations are essential to modernization. Aside from promoting efficiency and consistency, improved coordination could present an opportunity for state regulators to pool already scarce resources. Moreover, standardization provides consistent and uniform consumer protection for all policyholders irrespective of where the policyholder resides.

Under the state-based regulatory system, states should develop a requirement that market conduct regulation be performed according to the

Handbook, which would significantly improve the consistency of consumer protection across all states. Moreover, as part of the examination protocol, states should develop a process whereby information relevant to the same or similar statutory and regulatory requirements first be sought from another regulator before issuing a duplicative request to the insurer. States should adhere to a "lead state" concept for multi-state market conduct examinations in order to eliminate unnecessary and duplicative examinations.

Another factor that may augment the variability of rigor and professionalism from one state to another is the increasing dependence of state regulators on contract examiners to perform market conduct examinations. States should develop explicit standards and protocols to govern contract examiners including cost and schedule, education, professional background, training requirements, and appropriate ethical standards regarding conflict of interest, confidentiality, privacy and report drafting. State regulators should also develop a list of approved contract examiners based on an objective evaluation of expertise and training to examine specific issues or industry participants.

Rate Regulation

Recommendation: States should monitor the impact of different rate regulation regimes on various markets in order to identify rate-related regulatory practices that best foster competitive markets for personal lines insurance consumers. FIO will work with state regulators to establish pilot programs for rate regulation that seek to maximize the number of insurers offering such products.

An insurance rate determines the price at which an insurance policy or contract is sold. Insurers use rates to determine the premium due on a particular insurance policy: premium equals the rate multiplied by the number of units of insurance purchased. The rate typically reflects the risk characteristics of the purchaser of insurance.

Rate regulation originated in the late 19th century, when insurers gathered in "bureaus" to set rates because of the concern that price competition would bring the threat of insolvency ("destructive competition"). Rate regulation also evolved to allow insurers to exercise greater discretion when setting rates. Whereas states formerly set a "mandatory rate," regulation now is generally based on a legal standard, shared by all states, that the rate not be "inadequate, excessive, or unfairly discriminatory." Today, rate regulation principally addresses affordability. The evolving views on the manner of setting rates is reflected in the variety of processes through which states now permit insurers to file rates with the state regulator. (*See* Box 9). However, many empirical studies suggest rate regulation, particularly in auto and homeowner insurance, may adversely impact market supply resulting in higher prices and an increase in the market share of the residual market.[75]

Box 9: Forms of Rate Rewlation

States exercise varying degrees of rate regulatory authority. Listed from the least to most stringent, the different types of rate regulation include:

- *Open rating* Insurers establish rates for the products with a presumption that the rates satisfi· the state standard. The state regulator intervenes only in limited circumstances.
- *Use and Fide.* An insurer releases a product with certain rates, while also submitting a rate filing for review. The regulator can object or disallow the filed rate within a fixed number of days after the request to review. If the regulator does not object to or disallow the proposed rate within the allotted timeframe, the insurer can continue using the rate in the market. In some states, if the rate request is disallowed within the review timeframe, the insurer is required to rebate the premiums already collected.
- *File and Use* An insurer files a rate request with the state regulator who has a fixed amount of time to review the filing. If the regulator does not take action within the allotted timeframe, the rate is deemed approved and the insurer implements the rates in the market.
- *Prior Approval* An insurer files a rate request with the state regulator and cannot implement the proposed rates until approved by the regulator.

In 2011, 35 jurisdictions required a prior approval process for some lines of coverage, 37 jurisdictions utilized a file and use process, four jurisdictions utilised a flex band rating scheme, 16 jurisdictions required use and file process, and 33 jurisdictions had no filing requirements for commercial lines except upon demand of the regulator. States often use a particular approach for rates dependent upon the line of insurance.

In general, however, rates for personal lines typically receive a higher degree of scrutiny than commercial lines and, therefore, rates for personal lines are more likely to be required to go through a prior approval process.

Proponents for an open market system argue that prior approval rate regulation unnecessarily injects local political dynamics into a private economic market. Some argue more broadly that rate regulation artificially depresses prices, forcing insurers out of otherwise important markets and distorts the real cost of insurance. Supporters of strict rate regulatory authority argue that such regulation is critical for providing affordable and accessible insurance. Proponents of open market systems counter that, as an "open market" state, Illinois does not regulate base rates for affordability, but relies on the competitive market to impose discipline on prices and cite as evidence that more insurers participate in the Illinois P/C markets than in any other state.

The "open market" approach is not the only alternative to strict rate oversight. In 2011, Tennessee adopted a "flex band rating" approach for personal lines policies that allows insurers to impose rate increases within a range of 15 percent of the prior year's rate. In 2011, Connecticut extended for another two years a flex band rating (originally enacted in 2006) for personal lines that allows insurers to impose rate increases within a range of 6 percent of the prior year's rate. These recent developments may indicate a trend among the states to consider alternatives to strict rate regulation.

Rate regulation processes and protocols are fertile areas for experimentation by the states. With different states testing alternative approaches to rate oversight, states can evaluate the results in other jurisdictions and identify best practices. States pursuing enhanced competition and capacity in personal lines insurance markets have the option of pursuing moderate rate regulatory reforms on a limited or pilot basis to test the view that the burdens of rate regulation deter competition and reduce market capacity.

In making a determination regarding whether or how to implement a pilot program a number of factors may be considered. In order to define the factors state regulators may use to make such a determination, it is important to understand the characteristics of a competitive market that provide sufficient market discipline to maximize the number of insurers offering products to consumers. FIO has authority to monitor the affordability and accessibility of non-health insurance products to traditionally underserved communities. In the exercise of this authority, FIO will continue to monitor developments in the area of rate regulation and work with state regulators to identify best practices for implementation of pilot programs, as well as best practices for monitoring the impact of any change on consumer access to insurance.

Risk Classification

Recommendation: (1) States should develop standards for the appropriate use of data for the pricing of personal lines insurance; (2) states should extend regulatory oversight to vendors that provide insurance score products to insurers; (3) FIO will study and report on the manner in which personal information is used for insurance pricing and coverage purposes.

In determining the insurance rate applicable to particular customers, together with eligibility for coverage and class of service, insurers increasingly consider a myriad of data points to determine an individual consumer's risk profile. In the context of personal lines insurance products, this practice is familiarly known as "risk classification." Many P/C insurers generally rely upon these methodologies, for example, to place a customer in a particular rating tier, which can carry particularized coverage limits and premium prices.

The increasingly prevalent methodology for determining risk profiles for P/C personal lines is to rely on insurance scores. Insurance scores are typically generated by algorithms that consider a large number of data points, including an applicant's driving history, age, gender, zip code, marital status and credit score, or the components of a credit score. Some estimates indicate that, to one degree or another, the vast majority of auto insurers factor in credit scores, or components of a credit score, when determining applicable policy rates. The impact of applying these scores can be substantial. For example, some studies suggest that a driver with a poor credit score may pay 40 percent more in premiums.

Proponents of insurance scores argue that the more data an insurer can collect about an applicant, the more accurately the insurer can evaluate risks and price the policy. They also assert that the accurate pricing enabled by an insurance score reduces the cost shift in an insurance pool in which consumers with a lower risk profile subsidize the costs of individuals with a higher risk profile. These arguments are made with particular reference to individuals with high risk habits or jobs, or individuals who live in high risk communities. Proponents also contend that insurance scores actually increase insurance availability in high risk areas because, in the absence of the ability to price accurately, insurers would elect not to offer insurance in those areas at all.

Insurance scores, however, are controversial. Certain insurance score components, like a credit score, have a greater impact on the price quoted for certain consumers. For example, insurers may price personal line policies higher if the policyholder is unmarried, which raises concerns about whether certain life events, such as divorce or death of a spouse, or, as in the case of gay and lesbian couples, the legal inability to marry in many states, should be considered an appropriate basis for increasing the price of mandatory insurance policies. In addition, rating factors like education, occupation, and credit score, or the components of a credit score, may be correlated with race and thus it may appear that a greater percentage of racial minorities pay higher prices.

Personal auto insurance provides an example of how concerns regarding risk classification processes and methodologies can play out. Critics of insurance scoring practices have maintained that risk determinations should rely on factors that have a direct connection with driving ability or capacity. Accordingly, these critics support a number of reforms ranging from prohibiting the use of credit scores to requiring that premiums be based on driving record, miles driven, and driving experience.

Ultimately, insurance scoring or other risk classification systems may be important tools that allow insurers to charge higher rates to individuals who engage in riskier behavior. However, regulators and consumers should better understand the criteria and methodology by which insurers develop a policyholder's risk profile. The technical evolution of insurance pricing has been driven by advances in data mining and technological capability, and responsible use of these techniques that imposes higher prices on truly risky behavior should be permitted. However, simply because data may be available regarding consumers does not mean that any data is relevant to determining the insurance premiums they should pay.

With an ever-expanding universe of personal information available, important questions regarding boundaries or limitations on the use of that personal information should be answered in the context of insurance. Therefore, regulatory policy and practice must clarify that the criteria and methodologies actually used by insurers not rely on impermissible or discriminatory factors. Risk classification factors may be an appropriate subject for binding, uniform federal standards, particularly to the extent that insurance scoring methodologies involve factors that implicate rights secured under federal law.

In addition to developing and articulating standards concerning the proper use of data and methodologies of risk classification, state regulators should develop protocols for oversight of vendors — or insurers if the insurer develops the protocol for its own use — that provide the algorithms and data that render insurance scores and affect eligibility, tier and price of coverage. In most cases, the vendors that sell insurance score products and services to insurers are not subject to oversight by state regulators. The lack of transparency into the development of insurance scores prevents regulators — and the public from meaningfully evaluating not only a rate but also the process by which that rate has been determined.

Improved regulatory oversight of the insurance score vendors should be a priority for state regulators, including the development and adoption of an appropriate model law that will subject insurance score vendors to licensing and examination standards. In addition, FIO has authority to monitor the affordability and accessibility of non-health insurance products to traditionally underserved communities. In the exercise of this authority, HO will monitor state regulatory activity in this area and move for federal involvement if reasonable progress is not achieved in the near term. In support of its responsibility to monitor access to affordable insurance to traditionally underserved communities, HO will study the appropriate boundaries of use of personal information for insurance pricing and coverage purposes.

Box 10: Access of Native Americans to Insurance

Recommendation: HO will consult with 11-ibal leaders to identify alternatives to improve the accessibility and affordability of insurance on sovereign Native American and Tribal lands.

The United States has a unique legal and political relationship with Indian tribes and Alaska Native entities as provided by the U.S. Constitution, treaties, court decisions, and federal statutes. Generally, state insurance laws and regulation do not apply to policies sold in Indian Country. Regulatory authority, the power to develop insurance law and regulation, and the authority to operate tribally-owned insurance companies remains with Tribal governments. However, the majority of Tribal governments have not established specific insurance regulatory regimes, thereby leaving the responsibility with Tribal courts to determine the acceptable market conduct of an insurer or insurance professional on Tribal lands.

The absence of defined regulatory parameters presents a challenge for insurers considering the sale of conventional insurance products in Indian Country. Insurers point to the lack of a legal and regulatory framework as a reason for not conducting business in Indian Country. Despite the progress some organizations have made to provide access to affordable insurance in Indian Country, there remains a genuine need for additional insurance protection to limit business owners' and individuals' exposure to devastating losses from natural disasters or other unforeseen events, which in turn may hamper economic development. This is an area in which federal action may be warranted.

One possible course for consideration is to facilitate purchase of broader flood coverage. The Department of Homeland Security oversees the National Flood Insurance Program (NFIP), which is administered in part by the Federal Emergency Management Agency (FEMA). To be eligible to purchase flood coverage, FEMA requires that the property be located within a FEMA flood map zone or designated flood zone. However, many Tribal lands are not mapped by FEMA. FEMA estimates that fewer than 90 of the 566 federally recognized Tribes reside on lands mapped by the NFIP and are, therefore, eligible for participation in conventional NFIP coverage.

The Department of Housing and Urban Development (HUD) helped address this coverage gap by recognizing the need for an affordable flood program on tribal lands that have not been mapped. This privately offered policy covers up to $15,000 in damage for an insured property. In coastal areas, this flood policy pays regardless of whether the insurer has determined the cause of damage to be wind or water. Tribes have encouraged the federal government to facilitate the development of alternative insurance programs by allowing enhanced flexibility in federal programs that would provide more affordable coverage options, including an NFIP partnership with a Native American-owned insurance or risk retention enterprise.

HO will initiate a consultation with Tribal leaders, including tribally-owned risk pools, and involve relevant federal agencies and state regulators, with the objective of identifying alternative course, of action to improve the accessibility and affordability of insurance on sovereign Tribal lands.

Nonadmitted and Reinsurance Reform Act of 2010

Recommendation: FIO will continue to monitor state progress on implementation of Subtitle B of Title V of the Dodd-Frank Act, which requires states to simplify the collection of surplus lines taxes, and determine whether federal action may be warranted in the near term.

The Nonadmitted and Reinsurance Reform Act (NRRA) was enacted as part of the Dodd-Frank Act. Part I of the he NRRA, which took effect on July 21, 2011, reformed surplus lines insurance by streamlining the collection of taxes for multi-state surplus lines placements.

Surplus lines insurance provides coverage for businesses and consumers for risks that are not adequately insured by insurers licensed to do business in the given states. Surplus lines policies often cover one policyholder for property that the policyholder owns in multiple states. Prior to July 21, 2011, states typically taxed the premium on a pro rata basis according to the value of the insured risks located in the various states. The various states, however, have different surplus lines tax collection processes and offices, as well as different tax rates. Thus, there was great potential for confusion among producers paying surplus lines taxes for multi-state risks.

The NRRA prohibits any state other than "the home State of an insured" from requiring premium tax payments from nonadmitted insurers. The NRRA permits states voluntarily to "enter into a compact or otherwise establish procedures" for allocating premium taxes for nonadmitted insurance paid to the insured's home state. Absent a compact, states may only collect premium tax on the premium written in the home state. The NRRA also expresses the intention of Congress that states adopt nationwide uniform requirements, forms, and procedures to provide for the reporting, payment, collection, and allocation of premium taxes for nonadmitted insurance.

As of December 31, 2012, five states and Puerto Rico were participating in the Nonadmitted Insurance Multi-State Agreement (NIMA), which created a central clearinghouse for reporting, collecting, and allocating nonadmitted insurance premium taxes. No other states are operating in a tax allocation agreement. Nine states have entered into the Surplus Lines Insurance Multistate Compliance Compact (SLIMPACT), which would also create a tax payment clearinghouse and an allocation agreement. However, SLIMPACT will not become effective until ten states enter into the compact. Many other states simply enacted legislation authorizing the collection and retention of 100 percent of the nonadmitted insurance premium taxes for which the state is the home state of the insured.

Seven states (three of which entered SLIMPACT and four of which have entered no premium tax allocation agreement) are collecting nonadmitted insurance premium taxes at a pro-rata rate according to the locations of the multi-state risks. Nonetheless, these states are retaining 100 percent of the premium taxes. Finally, some states are taxing 100 percent of nonadmitted insurance premiums, including premiums for risks located in non-U.S. jurisdictions. Some question the legality of such a practice and suggest that it subjects insureds to double taxation.

The NRRA could be a model for insurance regulatory reform because it preserves state regulation but provides incentives for states to act in a manner consistent with federal guidelines. It urges states to simplify and make uniform the regulation of surplus lines insurance in the United States. However, the states have not fulfilled this vision as some states have agreed to share the premium tax collected from surplus lines insurance and others have opted to retain the premium tax applicable to the insurer's home state. A compact seems no more likely than before the NRRA became law. Implementation of the NRRA demonstrates the challenge of facilitating coordinated state action when coordinated action may materially impact state general revenue funds. FIO will continue to monitor state progress on this issue. Further federal action on this issue may be warranted in the near term.

Natural Catastrophes[76]

Recommendation: States should identify, adopt, and implement best practices to mitigate losses from natural catastrophes.[77]

Natural catastrophes can cause severe stress on all aspects of an affected community or region. These events strain P/C insurance markets. With an estimated $58 billion in insured losses in the U.S. resulting from weather events, 2012 surpassed the average insured losses of $27 billion from 2000 to 2011.[78] Large-scale natural catastrophes insured through the private sector strain industry resources, often resulting in higher premium rates for consumers. After significant outlays resulting from a natural catastrophe, insurers typically rebuild capital levels through increases in premiums, which often result in higher prices for consumers.

Higher premiums following a catastrophe can limit the affordability and accessibility of conventional insurance to consumers. When insurers raised premiums and curtailed dramatically offers of coverage following Hurricane Andrew in 1992 and after the Northridge earthquake in 1994, states created publicly supported or operated insurance or reinsurance programs to improve accessibility and affordability of property insurance coverage.

In a 2010 report, the GAO reviewed a sample of these public catastrophe programs, many of which have been growing over the last half of the decade.[79] From 2005-2010, the state insurance program in Mississippi had grown 495 percent, Texas had grown 147 percent, and Florida had grown 146 percent. The GAO found that some state catastrophe programs rely upon risk transfer through the reinsurance markets, while others rely on post-event funding, bonding, and assessments, to pay for incurred losses.

States also approach and design these residual market programs with different objectives. Some state programs encourage broad participation while other state programs attempt to manage participation through eligibility requirements, rates, or through other legislative or market-oriented approaches. Most states do not charge actuarially justified rates to residents seeking to participate in a state residual market program. In particular, the GAO found:

> Six of the 10 programs charged rates that did not fully reflect the risk of loss, potentially discouraging private market involvement and mitigation efforts by property owners. However, charging rates that do not fully reflect the risk of loss can also potentially increase broad-based participation in state programs. Officials from 7 of the 10 programs said that they took steps to encourage private market participation, and officials from 9 programs told us that they are implementing or considering ways to encourage mitigation, including providing mitigation credits or attempting to develop a more effective mitigation plan. Officials from most of the programs said they encourage broad participation in their programs; however, a few said they specifically discourage it and instead try to encourage homeowners to purchase insurance from the private market.[80]

The results of state involvement can be mixed and, accordingly, state approaches are evolving. The California Earthquake Authority (Authority) requires insurers writing homeowner policies either to offer earthquake coverage or to join and participate in the Authority. The Authority is privately funded and generally manages its exposure through the purchase of private reinsurance. While earthquake insurance is now available to California property owners, the premium cost appears prohibitive for most. Only approximately 14 percent of California property owners have earthquake insurance, penetration rates roughly the same as before the Northridge earthquake.

Industry critics assert that public insurance programs in some areas exposed to hurricanes may limit or crowd out private market capital. Nevertheless, states with coastal areas exposed to hurricanes have found that public support can improve the accessibility of homeowner insurance. Public sector programs frequently inject public capital into an insurance market at rates with which the private sector cannot compete.

The NFIP provides protection for property owners against losses caused by flooding. Superstorm Sandy illustrates the important role of the NFIP in supplementing coverage available for property owners through the private insurance market. Until 2005 and the devastating losses of Katrina, Rita, and Wilma, premiums collected by the NFIP effectively covered annual losses. Due to the hurricane losses of 2005, though, the NFIP accumulated a deficit in excess of $18 billion. When Superstorm Sandy hit the northeast in October 2012, NFIP owed the U.S. Treasury $17.8 billion. Due to losses from Sandy, Congress passed legislation increasing the borrowing authority of the NFIP to $30.4 billion.

The Biggert-Waters Flood Insurance Reform Act of 2012 modifies important provisions of the NFIP. First, premiums paid for NFIP coverage will more closely approximate rates justified by the risk of loss (*i.e.* more actuarially justified). Second, NFIP, for the first time, is authorized to secure reinsurance from the private market at rates and on terms determined to be reasonable and appropriate.[81]

At this time, different states are engaged in a variety of approaches that are sufficiently new and varied such that best practices for national adoption should wait until further development and identification of the more successful of these programs. While public policy debates are focused on the relative merits of residual market insurance programs, enhanced property owner mitigation initiatives receive widespread support. The amount of insured loss for a particular natural catastrophe is a function of the density of exposed properties in an area, and the ability of those properties to withstand the effects of the disaster. Effective mitigation strongly enhances the safety of occupants and the durability of property.

Empirical data supports the adoption of statewide building codes to save lives and to reduce the cost of property damage. A study by the Louisiana State University Hurricane Center estimated that stronger building codes would have reduced wind damage from Hurricane Katrina by 80 percent, saving as much as $8 billion. A more recent report, sponsored by the Federal Alliance for Safe Homes, a nonprofit organization focusing on economic resiliency and the role of mitigation in reducing the economic impact of natural disaster, used the uncommonly large number of natural disasters occurring in 2011 to highlight the important role that mitigation and planning have played as different areas recovered from natural disasters.[82]

While difficult to implement mitigation measures for every building in a catastrophe prone area, states and communities investing in the science of mitigation and exploring ways to reduce losses through construction standards may offer the best opportunity for ensuring access to affordable insurance. Proper construction techniques and materials can save lives and reduce both insured losses and taxpayer burden.

States should identify, adopt, and implement best practices for construction standards, including building codes, to mitigate losses from natural catastrophes. FIO intends to expound at greater length on issues involved with natural catastrophes in the forthcoming report required by the Biggert-Waters National Flood Insurance Reform Act of 2012.

V. Taking Account of Regulatory Reform

In June 2009, Treasury published the white paper entitled *Financial Regulatory Reform: A New Foundation*, which articulated six principles by which to measure proposals for insurance regulatory reform:[83]

1) Effective systemic risk regulation with respect to insurance.
2) Strong capital standards and an appropriate match between capital allocation and liabilities for all insurance companies.
3) Meaningful and consistent consumer protection for insurance products and practices.
4) Increased national uniformity through either a federal charter or effective action by the states.
5) Improve and broaden the regulation of insurance companies and affiliates on a consolidated basis, including those affiliates outside of the traditional insurance business.
6) Increased international coordination. Improvements to our system of insurance regulation should satisfy existing international frameworks, enhance the international competitiveness of the American insurance industry, and expand opportunities for the insurance industry to export its services.

The Dodd-Frank Act addresses some of these principles directly. For example, the Dodd-Frank Act provides a mechanism for consolidated supervision of insurance firms, or firms with insurance subsidiaries, by empowering the Council to determine that a nonbank financial company shall be supervised by the Federal Reserve if, at least in part, the firm's material financial distress could pose a threat to the financial stability of the United States. If the Council determines that supervision by the Federal Reserve is appropriate, then the firm shall also be subject to enhanced prudential standards. Designation of such firms allows for consolidated supervision of insurers, including corporate affiliates. Similarly, with respect to increased international coordination, Congress empowered FIO to represent the United States on prudential aspects of international insurance matters.

While not all of the six principles are directly addressed by the Dodd-Frank Act, as described more fully in this Report, those topics are the subject of current reform initiatives at both the national and international level. For example, supervisors worldwide are reviewing capital and consolidated supervision regimes independently and multilaterally, including the NAIC and the IAIS. Countries including Mexico, Canada, and China are implementing modernized insurance supervisory regimes. Consumer protection and market regulation also remains the subject of state, national and international attention. A summary of reform efforts with respect to each of the six principles is discussed below.

Systemic Risk Regulation

Title I of the Dodd-Frank Act establishes the Council and charges it with identifying risks to the financial stability of the United States, promoting market discipline, and responding to emerging threats to the stability of the United States financial system. Under Title I, the Council may determine that a nonbank financial company, including an insurer, shall be supervised by the Federal Reserve and shall be subject to prudential standards if the Council concludes that company's material financial distress or activities could pose a threat to the financial stability of the United States. This supervision, together with heightened prudential standards, will better allow regulators to address and mitigate risks to the financial stability of the United States posed by nonbank financial companies.

The Council has three members who specifically have background in or who are involved with oversight of the insurance sector. These members are:

(1) a voting member with insurance expertise, who is appointed by the President, with the advice and consent of the Senate; (2) the FIO Director, who is a non-voting member; and (3) a state insurance commissioner, also a non-voting member. This representation provides the Council with significant regulatory experience and knowledge of the insurance industry.

Insurance sector participants and observers argue that traditional insurance business activities do not present the kind of risk that could, in the event of failure, impair the functioning of the U.S. financial markets. This argument seeks to distinguish insurers from traditional financial intermediaries on the ground that insurers by and large do not rely on short-term funding and are not susceptible to runs or liquidity stresses because insurers do not hold liabilities, such as deposits. Ordinarily, a withdrawal from an insurer presupposes the occurrence of an event covered in a policy (*e.g.*, an accident or death). These events are typically uncorrelated (except in the event of mass catastrophes or disasters).

Financial stability concerns arise more often when traditional insurers engage in non-traditional activities, such as derivatives trading, securities lending, or other shadow banking activities, or when they offer products that have features that make them susceptible to runs. Through the Council's authority to determine that nonbank financial companies shall be subject to supervision by the Federal Reserve and enhanced supervision and prudential standards, the orderly liquidation authority with respect to failing firms that could threaten financial stability, and the comprehensive regulation of the derivatives markets, regulatory agencies now have much better tools to address threats to financial stability posed by any particular insurer. Reforms of solvency regulation discussed in this Report, moreover, would further strengthen the supervisors' ability to address risks posed by insurers to financial stability.

Capital Adequacy

As discussed more fully in this Report, capital adequacy standards for insurers are a subject currently being evaluated by the domestic and international insurance regulatory community. State regulators, through the NAIC's SMI initiative and in the EU-U.S. Insurance Project (*see* Box 4), are reviewing state-based RBC standards. Separately, but as a related matter, the IAIS ComFrame initiative will develop a quantitative capital standard for internationally active insurance groups. This Report's recommendations encourage not only further work on this front, but also improved uniformity and oversight across jurisdictions with respect to discretionary practices, more robust regulation of captives and special purpose vehicles, and better oversight of accreditation processes. These additional measures will be important steps toward modernizing capital adequacy standards in insurance regulation.

Meaningful and Consistent Consumer Protection

This Report identifies a number of areas for improving consumer protection. Areas such as producer licensing, product approval, and market conduct examinations are among the areas that have long been considered appropriate for improvement and modernization, particularly through establishment of uniform nationwide standards. This Report touches on these issues, and on others such as risk classification, rate regulation, natural catastrophes, and suitability for customers of annuities products.

National Uniformity

A uniform system of insurance regulation can reduce unnecessary cost and burden. A 2009 study by McKinsey & Co. estimated that regulatory costs added as a result of the current system total $13 billion annually, $7.2 billion of which are borne by P/C insurers.[84] Although many note that the states have taken significant steps towards improvement, the state regulatory system continues to suffer from a lack of uniformity. This Report has recognized uniformity as a central concern regarding the current system of insurance regulation in the United States and, throughout, the analysis and recommendations point to concrete measures to improve uniformity with respect to both solvency and market conduct regulation.

Consolidated Supervision

The Dodd-Frank Act introduces consolidated supervision of insurers in two different ways. First, to the extent an insurer or group is designated by the Council under Title I, its financial activities will be regulated as a consolidated entity. Second, in Title III, the Dodd-Frank Act eliminated OTS and turned oversight of federally chartered thrifts to the OCC, and made the Federal

Reserve Board the supervisor of thrift holding companies at the consolidated level, including those with insurance subsidiaries or affiliates.

Nevertheless, a substantial number of insurers are part of larger corporate groups that are not covered by either Title I or Title III of the Dodd-Frank Act. Accordingly, determining how best to introduce consolidated supervision has been an agenda item both for state regulators and international supervisors. Domestic efforts have met with mixed results, in part reflecting the inherent limits of state jurisdiction. This Report supports the state regulators' efforts to improve consolidated supervision practices. The Report also provides recommendations for the short term, including enhancement of supervisory colleges. Particularly in light of the global nature of the activities of large insurance firms, this is an important area for continuing work.

International Coordination

In Title V, the Dodd-Frank Act vests FIO with authority to coordinate and develop federal policy on prudential aspects of international insurance matters and to represent the United States at the IAIS. FIO today actively represents the United States in international fora, involvement that will continue to expand. At the IAIS, FIO serves on the Executive and Financial Stability Committees, and serves as Chair of the Technical Committee. FIO also serves on several of the IAIS subcommittees. FIO also consults and coordinates with state regulators and other federal agencies in connection with these activities. For example, FIO's collaboration with state regulators has brought the EU-U.S. Insurance Project to a defined path forward. Insurers operating on both sides of the Atlantic have increasing certainty about the impact of regulatory developments, and supervisors in both jurisdictions have heightened awareness and understanding of the other's regulatory regime.

Efforts at international coordination must also continue apace because many aspects of the insurance sector are increasingly global and standard-setting activities will deeply affect oversight of the industry in both developed and emerging markets around the world. Moreover, inattention to global matters and discord among jurisdictions could lead to competitive disadvantages for U.S. firms. Accordingly, this Report contains recommendations specifically tailored to cross-border matters, such as reinsurance, which have important competitive and solvency implications.

VI. CONCLUSION

It is not enough to say that the U.S. system of insurance regulation should be improved and modernized – this is true in every regulatory framework. Financial services evolve with great pace, and regulators of every sector are challenged to remain current, to foster competitive markets, and to protect consumers. Insurance does not differ from banking, securities and commodities in this respect – the insurance sector and its national and international markets are in constant flux.

This Report has identified some targeted and broad areas for which reform of the state-based system of insurance regulation is appropriate. Any reform proposal must also account for the threshold issue of how that reform will be achieved. Notwithstanding a decades-long debate about whether insurance should be regulated at the state or federal level, for the benefit of U.S.-based insurers and consumers, the debate is best reframed as one in which the question is where federal involvement is warranted, not whether federal regulation should completely displace state-based regulation.

Insurance markets are increasingly global, and any structural reform proposal should be premised on objective analyses of current regulation, identification of subject matter areas genuinely in need of reform, and the inherent legal and practical limits of the states. While this Report does not propose a recommendation for every conceivable shortcoming of the insurance industry and its regulatory framework, it sheds light on areas in need of prompt modernization and improvement.

With respect to prudential oversight, state-based regulation has largely evolved with the recognition that the ability of an insurer to pay a claim is the bedrock on which the U.S. insurance market is based. While not beyond reproach, and in need of specific reforms identified in this Report, state regulators have developed a system of entity-specific financial oversight that satisfies this most fundamental regulatory objective. States need to improve prudential oversight of insurers, but are working in that direction. FIO will monitor state regulatory developments, including those called for in this Report, and will present options for federal involvement as such options become necessary.

Any system with 56 independent jurisdictions is inherently limited in its ability to regulate uniformly and efficiently. This remains true for the state-based system of insurance regulation in the United States. The impact of this lack of uniformity is felt acutely in both prudential matters and in certain areas of marketplace oversight. To address the inefficiencies and lack of uniformity in the state regulatory system, federal involvement will be necessary. The *status quo*, or a state-only solution, will not resolve the problems of inefficiency, redundancy, or lack of uniformity, or adequately address issues of national interest. This Report describes some of those areas where federal standards and intervention may be most beneficial.

Working with all aspects of the insurance sector, including state regulators and policymakers, consumers and industry, FIO will recommend additional improvements to the U.S. system of insurance regulation that best integrate the interests of U.S. insurers and consumers. Whether, and to what extent, those improvements will require federal involvement will often depend upon the subject matter, circumstances, and ability and willingness of the states to resolve the underlying issue.

End Notes

[1] SNL Financial LC (April 25, 2013).

[2] *See* Department of Commerce, Bureau of Economic Analysis, http://www.bea.gov/national/index.htm#gdp (reporting – via the "Current-dollar and 'real' GDP" hyperlink – 2012 nominal GDP of $15,684.8 billion).

[3] Department of Labor, Bureau of Labor Statistics, http://data.bls.gov/timeseries/CES5552400001?data_tool=XGtable (data extracted on April 5, 2013).

[4] National Insurance Producer Registry (NIPR), *2012 Annual Report, 9, available at* http://www.nipr.com/doc-uments/2012_NIPR_Annual_Report.pdf.

[5] SNL Financial LC (April 25, 2013).

[6] Federal Deposit Insurance Corporation (FDIC), *Quarterly Banking Profile*, 7 (Fourth Quarter 2012), *available at* http://www2.fdic.gov/qbp/2012dec/qbp.pdf (reporting $14.5 trillion of total assets held by FDIC-insured institutions.

[7] SNL Financial LC (April 25, 2013) (the $6.8 trillion of invested assets includes separate account assets held by L/H insurers).

[8] AIG was regulated at the holding company level by the former Office of Thrift Supervision.

[9] For discussion of consolidated supervision of U.S. insurance groups, see: IMF, United States: *Publication of Financial Sector Assessment Program Documentation — Detailed Assessment of Observance of IAIS Insurance Core Principles (2010).*

[10] In the FIO Act, 31 U.S.C. § 313(r)(2), a "covered agreement" is defined as a "bilateral or multilateral agreement regarding prudential measures with respect to the business of insurance or reinsurance that – (A) is entered into between the United States and one or more foreign governments, authorities, or regulator entities; and (B) relates to the recognition of prudential measures with respect to the business of insurance or reinsurance that achieves a level of protection for insurance or reinsurance consumers that is substantially equivalent to the level of protection achieved under State insurance or reinsurance regulation."

[11] 31 U.S.C. § 313(p).

[12] 31 U.S.C. § 313(p)(3).

[13] McKinsey & Company, "Improving Property and Casualty Insurance Regulation In the United States," (April 2009).

[14] The Financial Services Roundtable, Public Comment on *How to Modernize and Improve the System of Insurance Regulation in the United States*, December 15, 2011, *available at* www.regulations.gov.

[15] *See* pp. 16-17.

[16] Susan Randall, *Insurance Regulation in the United States: Regulatory Federalism and the National Association of Insurance Commissioners*, Florida State University Law Review Vol. 26, 625 at 632 (citing 1995 NAIC Annual Report 1 (1996) (quoting Baltimore Underwriter, June 1871)).

[17] Kenneth J. *Meier, The Political Economy of Regulation: The case of insurance* (1988), pp. 57-8.

[18] Theodore Roosevelt's Annual Message to Congress for 1904; House Records HR 58A-K2; Records of the U.S. House of Representatives; Record Group 233; Center for Legislative Archives; National Archives.

[19] *New York Times,* "Bill for Government Control of Insurance; to be introduced in the Senate by John F. Dryden," Feb. 27, 1905, p. 5.

[20] *Id.*

[21] Louis D. Brandeis, Counsel for the Protective Committee of Policy-Holders of the Equitable Life Assurance Society, "Life Insurance: The abuses and the remedies," Address delivered before the Commercial Club of Boston, 1905, *available at* http://www.archive.org.

[22] *United States v. South-Eastern Underwriters Association*, 322 U.S. 533 (1944).

[23] *Id.* at 540. The Court noted that the "business is not separated into 48 distinct territorial compartments which function in isolation from each other. Interrelationship, interdependence, and integration of activities in all the states in which they operate are practical aspects of the insurance companies' methods of doing business."

[24] *Id.* at 552-553.

[25] The McCarran–Ferguson Act, 15 U.S.C. §§ 1011-1015.

[26] *Id.* at § 1012(b).

[27] Sen. Thomas J. Dodd, "High-Risk Automobile Insurance Company Insolvencies," *Congressional Record*, vol. 112, Feb. 17, 1966, pp. 3373-3374.

[28] The Federal Insurance Act (S. 3884, 1976). A modified version of the bill was introduced as S.1710 in the 95th Congress.

[29] U.S. House of Representatives, Committee on Energy and Commerce, Subcommittee on Oversight and Investigations, *Failed Promises: Insurance Company Insolvencies,* 101st Cong., 2nd Sess., Committee Print 101-P (Washington: GPO 1990).

[30] *Id.* at III.

[31] The Federal Insurance Solvency Act (H.R. 4900, 1992). The bill provided for a broad federal preemption of state insurance regulatory powers.

[32] U.S. House of Representatives, Committee on Energy and Commerce, Subcommittee on Oversight and Investigations, *Wishful Thinking: A World View of Insurance Solvency Regulation,* 103rd Cong,, 2nd Sess., Committee Print 103-R (Washington: GPO, 1994).

[33] *Id.*

[34] *Id.*, at 128.

[35] Pub.L. 106-102, (1999).

[36] *Id.* at § 321.

[37] NAIC NARAB (EX) Working Group Report: Certification of States for Producer Licensing Reciprocity, Adopted Aug. 8, 2002. In 2008, in 2009, and again in 2011, Members

introduced "NARAB II" bills to establish a national producer registry (H.R. 5611 (2008); H.R. 2554 (2009); H.R. 1112 (2011)). If enacted, the legislation would create NARAB as a national, nonprofit producer licensing corporation and would prohibit states from imposing any additional licensing requirements on non-resident producers who are NARAB members.

[38] State Modernization and Regulatory Transparency Act (Discussion draft authored by Rep. Oxley, Chairman, House Fin. Serv. Comm. and Rep. Baker, Chairman, Capital Markets Subcomm.) (2004) available at http://www.aba.com/ABIA/Pages/Issue_RM.aspx.

[39] S. 40 and H.R. 3200.

[40] *Id.* These proposals are sometimes described as "dual charter" proposals.

[41] Treasury, *Blueprint for a Modernized Financial Regulatory Structure*, March, 31, 2008.

[42] *Id.*

[43] The National Insurance Consumer Protection Act (H.R. 1880) (April 2, 2009).

[44] *Id.*

[45] Treasury, *Financial Regulatory Reform: A New Foundation: Rebuilding Financial Supervision and Regulation*, June 2009, at 39.

[46] American International Group, Inc., Form 10-K, 2007.

[47] American International Group, Inc., Form 10-Q, Q2, 2008.

[48] Congressional Oversight Panel June Oversight Report: *The MG Rescue, Its Impact an Markets, and the Government's Exit Strategy* (June 10, 2010).

[49] NAIC, *Annual Statement Permitted and Prescribed Practices Reports* (http://www.naic.org/index_pps.htm).

[50] SNL Financial (data extracted May 20, 2013) (comparing "Policyholder Surplus: State Prescribed & Permitted Practices" with "Policyholder Surplus: NAIC Statutory Accounting Principle" data elements at the "SNL Group" level for 2008 annual data).

[51] State regulators developed the Financial Regulation Standards Accreditation Program (*see* p. 29) between 1988 and 1990 in the midst of a series of large insolvencies and congressional inquiry into those insolvencies that culminated in the *Failed Promises* report.

[52] 31 U.S.C. § 313(c)(1)(E).

[53] *See* IAISweb.org for more details.

[54] Marsh, Next Generation Captives – Optimising Opportunities, 2008; A.M. Best Captive Center.

[55] Business Insurance, Market Insights, Captive Domiciles 2012.

[56] This refers to the counterparty credit risk associated with a reinsurer paying an insurer for the insurer's incurred losses.

[57] Reinsurance Association of America, Offshore Reinsurance in the U.S. Market – 2011 Data (2012).

[58] *See AIA v. Garamendi,* 539 U.S. 982, 124 S. Ct. 35 (2003).

[59] "Covered agreement" is defined at 31 U.S.C. §314 (*See* footnote 10).

[60] IMF, United States: *Publication of Financial Sector Assessment Program Documentation — Detailed Assessment of Observance of IAIS Insurance Core Principles (2010).*

[61] Financial Stability Board, Press Release, Meeting of the Financial Stability Board in Zurich on 28 January (2013).

[62] Both the FDI Act and the Orderly Liquidation Authority in Title II of the Dodd-Frank Act provide for a temporary 24-hour automatic stay.

[63] Not all insurance lines are covered by guaranty funds, including financial guaranty, mortgage insurance, and title insurance. Some states also exempt health maintenance organizations (HMOs) requiring solvent HMOs operating in the state to assume the policies and enrollees

of the insolvent HMO. Additionally, some insurance companies offer non-insurance, non-annuity products such as guaranteed investment contracts (GICs) which are also not covered by guaranty funds.

[64] However, see Box 3: Assistance to the Insurance Industry during the Financial Crisis.

[65] 133 S. Ct. 2694 (2013).

[66] *Id.* at 2693.

[67] Indexed annuities do not have segregated accounts. Indeed, the insurer may not actually invest in the instruments associated with the underlying rate or index, such as the securities that correspond to the selected securities index.

[68] In 1959, the Supreme Court decided that variable annuities are securities.

[69] The Model Suitability Regulation was first adopted in 2003 and applied only to sales to seniors. It was revised in 2006 to apply to all consumers. The model regulation was revised again in 2010. The term Model Suitability Regulation is used here to refer to the 2010 version.

[70] *See* Section 989A

[71] *See* Section 989J, 15 U.S.C. § 77c(a) (8).

[72] Insurance Regulation, Preliminary Views on States' Oversight of Insurers' Market Behavior, May 6, 2003.

[73] The NAIC developed a number of tools states may use to share information and coordinate market conduct regulation activity. In addition to Market Conduct Annual Statement, these include the Market Initiative Tracking System, the Special Activities Database, the Complaints Database System, the Examination Tracking System, Market Analysis Review System, and Regulatory Information Retrieval System.

[74] *See* NAIC Market Regulation and Consumer Affairs Committee *Market Regulation Survey* August 3, 2012.

[75] *See* Lauren Regan, Sharon Tennyson, and Mary Weiss *The Relationship Between Auto Insurance Rate Regulation and Insured Loss Costs: An Empirical Analysis*, NAIC 2009; Mary Weiss, Sharon Tennyson, and Laureen Regan *The Effect of Regulated Premium Subsidies on Insurance Costs: An Empirical Analysis of Automobile Insurance,* The Journal of Risk and Insurance, Vol. 77, No. 3, 2010; Richard Derrig and Sharon Tennyson *The Impact of Rate Regulation on Claims: Evidence from Massachusetts Automobile Insurance*, Risk Management and Insurance Review, 2011, Vol. 14, No. 2, 173-199; and Sharon Tennyson, *The Long-Term Effects of Rate Regulatory Reforms in Automobile Insurance Markets*, Insurance Research Council, March 2012.

[76] Pursuant to the Biggert-Waters Flood Insurance Reform Act, Pub.L.112-141; 126 Stat. 916 (2012), FIO will submit a report to Congress on a variety of insurance-related natural catastrophe topics.

[77] This section does not address terrorism risk or the Terrorism Risk Insurance Act (TRIA), as renewed and set to terminate on December 31, 2014. The President's Working Group on Financial Markets is studying and will issue a report on TRIA.

[78] Munich Re, 2012 Natural Catastrophe Year in Review, January 3, 2013, *available at* http://www.munichreamerica.com/webinars/2013_01_natcatreview/natcat_webinar_record/player.html2012.

[79] GAO, *Natural Catastrophe Insurance Coverage Remains a Challenge for State Programs*, GAO-10-568R Natural Catastrophe Insurance Coverage (2010).

[80] *Id.* p. 3.

[81] 42 U.S.C. § 4055(a)(2).

[82] "Impact 2011: Examining a Year of Catastrophes through the Lens of Resiliency," December 2011, prepared by Weather Predict Consulting, Inc. for the Federal Alliance for Safe Homes 2011 Annual Meeting, www. flash.org.

[83] Treasury, *Financial Regulatory Reform, A New Foundation: Rebuilding Financial Supervision and Regulation*, June 2009, at 39.

[84] McKinsey & Company, April 2009, *supra*.

In: Modernizing U.S. Insurance Regulation … ISBN: 978-1-63484-338-6
Editor: Willard Vasquez

Chapter 2

THE BREADTH AND SCOPE OF THE GLOBAL REINSURANCE MARKET AND THE CRITICAL ROLE SUCH MARKET PLAYS IN SUPPORTING INSURANCE IN THE UNITED STATES*

Federal Insurance Office

GLOSSARY

A/H	Accident & Health Insurance
BCR	Basic Capital Requirement
CEA	California Earthquake Authority
ComFrame	Common Framework for the Supervision of IAIGs
Council	Financial Stability Oversight Council
Dodd-Frank Act	Dodd-Frank Wall Street Reform and Consumer Protection Act
FAA	Federal Aviation Administration
FCIC	Federal Crop Insurance Corporation
FEMA	Federal Emergency Management Agency
FHCF	Florida Hurricane Catastrophe Fund

* This is an edited, reformatted and augmented version of a report issued by the U.S. Department of the Treasury, December 2014 and updated February 2015.

FIO	Federal Insurance Office
FIO 2014 Annual Report	U.S. Department of the Treasury, *Federal Insurance Office Annual Report on the Insurance Industry* (2014)
FRN	Federal Register Notice of June 27, 2012
FSB	Financial Stability Board
G-SII	Global Systemically Important Insurer
GWP	Gross Written Premiums
HLA	Higher Loss Absorbency
IAIG	Internationally Active Insurance Group
IAIS	International Association of Insurance Supervisors
ILS	Insurance-Linked Securities
ILW	Industry Loss Warranty
LAE	Loss Adjustment Expenses
L/H	Life & Health Insurance
Model Law	NAIC Credit for Reinsurance Model Law and Regulation
Modernization Report	Department of the Treasury, *How to Modernize and Improve the System of Insurance Regulation in the United States* (December 2013)
NAIC	National Association of Insurance Commissioners
NFIP	National Flood Insurance Program
NRRA	Nonadmitted and Reinsurance Reform Act of 2010
NWP	Net Written Premiums
OPIC	Overseas Private Investment Corporation
P/C	Property & Casualty Insurance
PHS	Policyholders' Surplus
Project	EU-U.S. Insurance Project
SPV	Special Purpose Vehicle
Treasury	U.S. Department of the Treasury
TRIA	Terrorism Risk Insurance Act of 2002, as amended
TRIP	Terrorism Risk Insurance Program
USTR	United States Trade Representative

I. INTRODUCTION

By premium volume, the United States is the largest single-country insurance market in the world. Insurers operating in the United States rely on reinsurers, both foreign and domestic, to support the issuance of new policies, to minimize fluctuations in loss experience, and to limit and diversify individual and portfolio risks, particularly in the case of catastrophes and natural disasters.

Reinsurance is a contract of indemnity between commercial parties – an insurer (i.e., the "cedent" or "ceding insurer") and one or more "assuming insurers" (i.e., reinsurers) – by which, in exchange for a premium, a specified portion of the risks under one or more insurance policies written by the cedent are transferred ("ceded") to the reinsurers. Reinsurance serves a variety of functions, and can be tailored to the particular needs of a given cedent. Reinsurance is commonly purchased to limit an insurer's loss experience resulting from insured risk exposures, to increase an insurer's underwriting capacity, to promote more efficient allocation of an insurer's capital, or to facilitate an insurer's entry to or exit from a particular line of business or market segment. Reinsurance serves an important function as protection for cedents against the accumulation of losses from a natural disaster or other catastrophe. "The reinsurance of peak risks originally assumed by primary insurers – i.e., risks with low probabilities of occurrence, but high severities – is the core business of reinsurers."[1]

The global reinsurance market includes organizations and companies that have operated for a century or more, as well as relatively new companies and alternative forms of risk transfer. The U.S. reinsurance sector continues to be an important source of capacity for domestic insurers seeking reinsurance. Non-U.S. reinsurers also play a key role, as U.S. insurers purchase a substantial amount of reinsurance protection from companies domiciled outside of the United States, or which are part of groups headquartered outside of the United States, including in Europe, the Asia-Pacific region, Bermuda, and other jurisdictions. Additionally, in recent years, insurers, reinsurers, and various capital market participants have developed a range of insurance-linked securities and special purpose vehicles, which have a growing role in the global risk transfer market.

The manner in which reinsurance is regulated in the United States depends upon whether or not the reinsurer is licensed in a U.S. state. Licensed reinsurers are subject to the same state-based regulation as other licensed insurers. Unlicensed reinsurers (typically non-U.S. companies) assuming risks from U.S. ceding insurers are indirectly regulated by state laws, including those that compel licensed insurers to obtain qualifying collateral from unlicensed reinsurers in order for the licensed insurers to take financial statement credit for liabilities ceded to such unlicensed reinsurers. Due to the global diversification of the industry, many non-U.S. reinsurers assuming risk from U.S. insurers are affected by such requirements.

Title V of the Dodd-Frank Wall Street Reform and Consumer Protection Act (Dodd-Frank Act),[2] established the Federal Insurance Office (FIO) in the U.S. Department of the Treasury (Treasury). Among other provisions, the Dodd-Frank Act authorizes FIO to monitor all aspects of the insurance industry,[3] which includes the reinsurance industry, and to coordinate federal efforts and develop federal policy on prudential aspects of international insurance matters, including matters relating to reinsurance.

This report has been prepared pursuant to the requirement under the Dodd-Frank Act for FIO to issue a report "describing the breadth and scope of the global reinsurance market and the critical role such market plays in supporting insurance in the United States" (Report).[4] In support of this Report, on June 27, 2012, Treasury published a notice in the Federal Register (FRN) seeking comments from interested parties. Thirty written comments from domestic and international parties were received, including from insurers, reinsurers, industry trade associations, and consumer advocates.[5] In addition, FIO consulted with a number of reinsurers, industry representatives, and other organizations throughout 2013 and 2014.

This Report describes the important role of the global reinsurance market in supporting the insurance industry in the United States. It is not the purpose of this Report to analyze the extent to which reinsurance or any particular reinsurer could be systemically important. Global reinsurance providers play a vital role supporting insurance in the United States, but by any metric, reinsurance constitutes only a comparatively minor component of the insurance industry. For example, global reinsurance premiums are only a small fraction of direct insurance premiums (less than 5 percent); and reinsurer assets are a small fraction of overall insurance industry assets.[6] Many global reinsurers and other capital market industry participants operate in the reinsurance market, demonstrating a high degree of substitutability and mobility of risk transfer capital.

II. BRIEF HISTORY OF REINSURANCE

Reinsurance has been practiced as a commercial endeavor for centuries.[7] Published references to reinsurance are found in English and European laws from the 15th, 16th, and 17th centuries.[8] For example, a translation from the *Guidon de la Mer* (Normandy, 1671) states:

> But if an underwriter repent of what he has done; if he be afraid to encounter the risk he has engaged to run, or find that he has incautiously bound himself to a greater amount than he may be able to discharge, he may shift it, or part of it, from himself to other insurers by causing a re-insurance to be made on the same risk, upon the best terms he can, and the new insurers will be responsible to him in case of loss, to the amount of the re-insurance.[9]

One author surmised that "[r]einsurance almost certainly grew out of the practice of offering risk to more than one insurer when the first insurer could not accept it all."[10] Prior to the American Revolutionary War, reinsurance for the fledgling American insurance industry was primarily provided through Lloyd's—an insurance market in London with roots dating to 1688 (Box 1). Access to Lloyd's was not available to the U.S. market, however, during the American Revolutionary War and in the very early years of the nation.[11] By the first quarter of the 19th century, some reinsurance business was being conducted by U.S. companies,[12] but it appears that most reinsurance was at that time placed overseas.[13] Reinsurance was well-established as an industry in the United States by the early 20th century.[14]

Concurrently, the modern global reinsurance industry developed during the 18th and 19th centuries. Cologne Re was founded in Germany as the first professional reinsurance company in 1842.[15] In the following decades, additional reinsurers were established throughout Europe, including Swiss Re in 1863 and Munich Re in 1880. Some of these companies continue to operate globally to this day, including as reinsurers of U.S. insurers.

Box 1: Lloyd's of London

The market now known as Lloyd's of London began conducting business from Edward Lloyd's coffee house in 1688. It is among the world's oldest suppliers of reinsurance, and has had a longstanding role as a supplier of reinsurance to U.S. insurers.

Lloyd's has a structure unique in the insurance industry: it is organized as a marketplace where underwriting "members" (the risk-bearing capital suppliers), now primarily consisting of corporations and insurance groups, including U.S.-based insurers, join together and provide capital to "syndicates" that underwrite risk. Presently, 91 syndicates operate within Lloyd's and underwrite a wide variety of insurance and reinsurance lines.

Syndicates are essentially annual joint ventures; members have the right, but not the obligation, to participate the following year. Managing agents, engaged by members to operate one or more syndicates, provide management, support staff, and the business infrastructure to individual syndicates. Business at Lloyd's must be placed through an accredited Lloyd's broker. Oversight of the market is conducted by the Corporation of Lloyd's, which sets capital standards, reviews and analyzes the activities of syndicates, and provides various other monitoring functions.[16]

During the first half of the 20th century, in large part due to the world wars, new reinsurers began to emerge in the United States as well as in countries (e.g., Switzerland) which experienced fewer commercial disruptions during the wars.[17] On the eve of World War II, to demonstrate its ability to reliably service U.S. business, Lloyd's set up an American trust fund to receive all dollar-denominated premiums and from which claims could be satisfied.[18] That fund evolved into the "Lloyd's American Trust Fund" and related funds established to secure the liabilities of its underwriting syndicates.[19]

In the early post-war years, state insurance regulators began to consider whether and how to develop uniform accounting treatment for reinsurance business ceded by U.S. insurers. The subject was still under discussion over 30 years later when, in 1982, the Illinois Department of Insurance submitted a report to the National Association of Insurance Commissioners (NAIC) proposing development of a model law to "create consistent financial standards for assuming reinsurers from state to state, accounting for reinsurance transactions and reserve credits ... and financial reporting and disclosure of certain reinsurance transactions."[20] In June of 1984, the NAIC adopted its Credit for Reinsurance Model Law and Regulation (the Model Law), which eventually formed the basis for the laws in all states requiring that non-U.S. reinsurers provide 100 percent collateralization of reinsurance liabilities to U.S. cedents in order for the cedents to receive regulatory "credit" for the reinsurance. The NAIC recently adopted amendments to the Model Law, which, if enacted as state law, would permit the state insurance regulator to grant full credit for reinsurance with reduced collateral under some circumstances.[21]

During the latter part of the 20th century, few new U.S.-based reinsurers were established despite the economic growth during the period. Bermuda, however, emerged as an international reinsurance center during this period.[22] Over the past two decades, the formation of Bermuda-domiciled reinsurance companies has occurred in waves corresponding to cyclical pricing patterns that followed the depletion of worldwide reinsurance capital in the property & casualty (P/C) sector due to extraordinarily large loss events.[23] These include the so-called class of 1992-1993 (following Hurricane Andrew); class of 2001-2002 (following the terrorist attacks of September 11, 2001); and the class of 2005-2006 (following Hurricanes Katrina, Rita, and Wilma).[24] New "classes" of traditional reinsurers did not emerge following record catastrophe losses in 2011 and Superstorm Sandy in 2012. Bermuda is now also becoming prominent in the alternative risk transfer market, discussed below.

Today, the reinsurance industry supporting the U.S. direct insurance market is global in scope, and primarily consists of approximately 50 large, professional reinsurers and reinsurance groups, as well as many smaller reinsurers.[25] According to analysis by the Reinsurance Association of America, in 2013 approximately $46 billion in total (P/C) reinsurance premiums were ceded by U.S.-based insurers to unaffiliated reinsurers; of this amount, approximately $28.4 billion of premiums were ceded to non-U.S. reinsurers and approximately $17.6 billion of premiums were ceded to U.S. professional reinsurers.[26] As addressed below, if the domiciles of ultimate parent companies are taken into account, the figures show that an even greater portion of U.S. reinsurance premiums are ceded to non-U.S. reinsurance groups.

Related market participants, including brokers and ancillary service providers, also contribute to the availability and affordability of reinsurance. In addition, new reinsurers and other vehicles to distribute insurance risks world-wide continue to be formed. Notably, capital from alternative sources (e.g., pension funds) has emerged to support new sources of risk transfer for insurance companies. In the first quarter of 2014, for example, sponsors issued some $1.6 billion of insurance-linked securities—a single quarter record. The majority of this "alternative capital" supports catastrophe bonds ("cat bonds"), a mechanism by which insurers securitize catastrophe risk.[27]

Capital in the reinsurance sector has generally been increasing year-over-year for most of the past decade. Aon Benfield reports that global reinsurance capital amounts to $570 billion as of mid-2014 (Figure 1).[28] Of this amount,

$511 billion is classified as traditional capital and $59 billion as alternative capital.

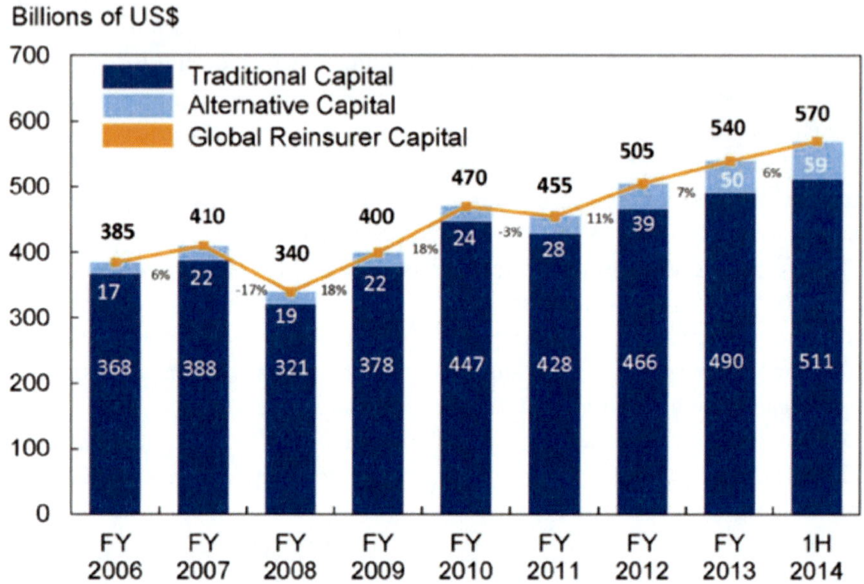

Source: Aon Benfield, The Aon Benfield Aggregate – Results for the Six Months Ended June 30, 2014.

Figure 1. Global Reinsurer Capital.

III. Definition and Forms of Reinsurance

A. Reinsurance Defined

Reinsurance is often described as "insurance of insurance companies."[29] It is a commercial agreement whereby one company (the reinsurer) indemnifies another (the cedent) for insurance losses under policies of insurance issued by the cedent. In a manner broadly analogous to how a policyholder is protected from loss by transferring risk to an insurer, under a reinsurance contract the cedent is protected from its own exposure to loss by transfer of the specified insurance risk to a reinsurer.

"Indemnity" is a fundamental characteristic of traditional reinsurance. In the context of reinsurance an indemnity contract is one in which a party (the reinsurer) only becomes obligated to reimburse (indemnify) the other after that party (the cedent) has itself incurred and paid a loss which is both covered by its own insurance policy or policies and within the scope of the reinsurance contract between the two parties.[30]

Essential elements of the reinsurance relationship therefore include: (1) a contract between at least two insurance companies, i.e., the cedent and the reinsurer(s); (2) one or more underlying insurance contracts, i.e., the policy or policies issued by the cedent to its own policyholders; and (3) a transfer of some insurance risk from the cedent to the reinsurer(s) pursuant to the contract of reinsurance.[31]

A reinsurance contract is formed only between a cedent and one or more reinsurers, whereas the underlying insurance policies are contracts between the cedent and its policyholders. The underlying policyholders are not parties to the reinsurance contract and generally do not have rights or obligations under it. Similarly, the reinsurer is not party to the underlying insurance policies, and does not have rights or obligations thereunder. In its role as direct insurer, the cedent has and maintains the obligation to adjust and, where appropriate, to pay the claims of its policyholders. Reinsurance does not alter those obligations or shift them to others, because privity of contract does not exist between the reinsurer and the cedent's policyholders.[32]

Accordingly, an insurer must "fulfill the terms of its policy whether or not it has reinsurance or whether or not the reinsurer is rightly or wrongly refusing to perform."[33]

Reinsurers themselves may also buy reinsurance protection (e.g., to address loss exposure from reinsurance contracts), called "retrocessions." The ceding reinsurer, or "retrocedent," redistributes some of the reinsurance risk it has assumed (from its cedents) through contracts with one or more other reinsurers, or "retrocessionaires." A reinsurer may also pool risks from several different affiliates and purchase a retrocession program that covers such risks placed by the reinsurance group on a more efficient basis.[34]

B. Forms of Reinsurance

Reinsurance is available for numerous lines of insurance business, both life and non-life, and the parties to a reinsurance contract have considerable discretion over the form and substance of an agreement, subject to certain regulatory restrictions imposed on the cedent. With some variation, however, reinsurance agreements generally take one of two basic forms, either "treaty" or "facultative" agreements. These two forms of reinsurance contracts are described below.

1. Treaty Reinsurance

A reinsurance treaty is a standing reinsurance agreement; in exchange for an agreed premium, the treaty covers a class of insurance risks specified in the contract. Typically the "cession" of the reinsured business by the cedent and the assumption of that business by the reinsurer are obligatory pursuant to treaty terms. That is, under treaty reinsurance premium and losses associated with the covered risks are automatically covered by the agreement to be transferred to one or more reinsurers—the reinsurer does not analyze the reinsured business on a policy-bypolicy basis before accepting the risk cession.[35] As compared to facultative reinsurance, addressed below, treaty reinsurance is less labor-intensive to place and administer, and is the more common form used.

Treaty reinsurance highlights the close business relationship and high degree of trust that customarily has existed between cedents and reinsurers. Reinsurers must "follow the fortunes" of the cedent – which means reinsurers are to a large degree bound by the fortuities of the underlying insurance business – even when reinsurers do not have an advance opportunity to evaluate individual risks underwritten by the insurer. For that reason, reinsurers must rely on the cedent to make sound underwriting and claims-management decisions which, in turn, benefit cedent and reinsurer alike. In this sense, cedents and treaty reinsurers have traditionally operated with mutual interests and objectives and, historically, the reinsurance relationship has been considered one of "utmost good faith."[36]

Reinsurance treaties are typically classified as either "pro rata" or "excess of loss" contracts. The decision whether to purchase a pro rata or an excess of loss reinsurance treaty depends on the cedent's objectives. In practice, both types of treaty reinsurance agreements are often purchased in combination to form an insurer's reinsurance program. For example, an insurer may purchase pro rata treaties and per risk excess of loss treaties in multiple layers, the benefits of which may reduce the risks exposed to its catastrophe per event treaties (described below). Such customization of different types of reinsurance across various lines of business allows an insurer to address its specific risk management concerns.

a. Pro Rata Reinsurance

For risks subject to a pro rata treaty, the insurer and reinsurer share premiums and exposures to losses in an agreed proportion. Pro rata reinsurance has the advantage of simplicity in design and administration, but may come at a relatively high cost to the cedent in terms of underwriting income and total return (as compared to excess of loss reinsurance). This form of reinsurance is particularly suited to addressing a cedent's need to ensure it has sufficient surplus for the business that it wishes to write, and is useful when a cedent is entering or exiting lines of business.[37]

Pro rata reinsurance treaties may be further classified as either "quota share" or "surplus share." Under a quota share treaty (commonly referred to as "coinsurance" in the life insurance context), the cedent and reinsurer share a predetermined percentage of both the premium charged for the underlying insurance policies and the exposure thereunder to first-dollar losses. For example, in a 25 percent quota share treaty, the reinsurer would receive 25 percent of the premiums and be liable to the insurer for 25 percent of the losses paid by the insurer as well as, generally, the same percentage of the insurer's loss adjustment expenses (LAE). In the event of loss, the insurer remains liable to its policyholders, but the insurer (as cedent) would be indemnified by the reinsurer for 25 percent of the amount of the covered loss and LAE paid under any reinsured policy. A surplus share treaty is similar to a quota share, but the cedent retains a fixed dollar amount of liability and cedes to the reinsurer a percentage of loss above that amount. Unlike a quota share treaty, therefore, the percentage of sharing between the insurer and reinsurer varies according to the limits of the underlying policy.

Pro rata treaties provide the cedent with "surplus relief" and the capacity to write more business or at larger limits. Regulatory-based accounting rules generally provide that insurers must recognize premium revenues as earned over the duration of a policy. In contrast, acquisition costs – primarily commissions paid to agents at policy inception – are expensed immediately. One result is that the insurer's reported regulatory-based capital in its financial statements is reduced at the inception and early stages of an insurance contract. A ceding commission, paid by the reinsurer to the cedent under a pro rata reinsurance agreement, can be immediately recognized by the cedent as income for regulatory accounting purposes and can therefore partially offset the burden of expensing up-front acquisition costs associated with obtaining the original insurance business.[38]

b. Excess of Loss Reinsurance

In contrast to pro rata reinsurance, excess of loss reinsurance is a form of protection against insured losses sustained above a predetermined and stated threshold, known as the cedent's "retention,"[39] and thus does not create a proportional sharing of risk. A reinsurer also may require a cedent to co-participate for a portion of losses above the retention so that the cedent has additional "skin in the game." Under excess of loss reinsurance, a cedent may choose to purchase coverage attaching at high levels of loss, thereby obtaining protection for a relatively modest premium. By indemnifying the insurer for losses above a specified level, excess of loss treaties help stabilize the net losses (i.e., after reinsurance recoveries) in an insurer's portfolio.

Excess of loss treaties generally take one of three forms: "per occurrence" excess of loss, "aggregate" excess of loss, or "per risk" excess of loss. Per occurrence excess of loss treaties protect a cedent from the accumulation of multiple policy losses arising from a single event. Thus, the cedent's retention will usually be much larger than its exposure under any policy that is subject to the treaty. Property catastrophe treaties, for example, are designed to protect against cumulative losses under multiple policies caused by a single natural disaster or other large-scale loss event.

Aggregate excess of loss treaties protect against the accumulation of losses over the effective period of the reinsurance contract. Under an aggregate excess of loss treaty, the reinsurer will indemnify the insurer for a share of losses that exceed an agreed dollar amount or other agreed metric (such as percentage of aggregate net premiums). This form of reinsurance is also called "stop-loss" reinsurance.

Per risk (or per policy) excess of loss treaties provide protection above an insurer's retention on individual risks or policies, rather than on an accident, event, or aggregate basis. The reinsurance contract will specify the class or type of business covered, and the retention and limit of the reinsurance contract will apply to each covered risk.

2. Facultative Reinsurance

Unlike treaty reinsurance, facultative reinsurance does not result in an automatic cession of risk by the cedent, nor an automatic acceptance of risk by a reinsurer. Instead, facultative reinsurance permits an insurer to decide which specific insured risks will be submitted to a reinsurer for consideration. Upon such submission, the reinsurer has the opportunity to underwrite the individual risk, and may elect to accept or decline such risk. Facultative reinsurance may create greater administrative burdens on both cedents and reinsurers because potential risk cessions must be analyzed on an individual basis rather than in advance as a book of business. As with treaty reinsurance, facultative reinsurance may be structured as either excess of loss or pro rata, depending upon the needs of the cedent. Though insurers have a variety of reasons for using facultative reinsurance, it is generally purchased for large or unusual risks, which may be wholly or partially outside the scope of a cedent's treaty arrangements.[40]

IV. The Purpose and Importance of Reinsurance

A. Uses of Reinsurance

Reinsurance is an important mechanism by which an insurer manages risk and the amount of capital it must hold to support such risk. Some of the more common purposes for reinsurance are highlighted below. Inasmuch as reinsurance is a business-to-business transaction, the purpose and terms of reinsurance contracts can vary greatly based upon the parties' needs and commercial objectives. Accordingly, this list is not an exhaustive recitation of the purposes for which insurers purchase reinsurance, but is intended to illustrate the range of benefits reinsurance provides to cedents and to the insurance sector in the United States.[41]

1. Stabilizing Underwriting Results

In order to offer products that cover risks faced by policyholders, an insurer generally must set prices (i.e., premiums) for its products before the "cost of goods sold" (i.e., claims) are known. For some coverages, it can take years — even decades — for all of the claims pertaining to a particular policy year to fully develop. The business of insurance is inherently susceptible to fluctuations in underwriting gains and losses, which can adversely affect an insurer's financial position.

Reinsurance can mitigate the risk of fluctuations in underwriting gains and losses faced by insurers. For example, insurers with significant exposures to catastrophic losses utilize reinsurance to help manage the extent of losses from a single event. Insurers often use reinsurance to limit potential losses from an individual policy or on an entire portfolio of policies ("book of business"), thereby tempering the adverse impacts of volatility.

2. Increasing Underwriting Capacity

To honor policy obligations, meet credit rating agency expectations, and comply with state-based regulatory requirements, insurers are required to hold capital. Regulatory requirements and potential loss levels that may significantly reduce or encumber capital may limit the ability of insurers to write increased, or even existing, levels of business, or to write policies with large limits.

Reinsurance addresses these challenges in at least two ways. First, reinsurance allows the insurer to transfer portions of the resulting risk to one or more reinsurers. For accounting purposes, the cedent's transfer of risk is recognized as a reduction of the cedent's policy liabilities (if the insurer has not yet paid the underlying policy claim) or as an asset (if the insurer has already paid the claim). The extent to which the receivable asset increases or the policy liabilities decrease, known as "credit for reinsurance," increases the cedent's reported policyholders' surplus (PHS), i.e., the insurer's assets less its liabilities as measured by regulatory accounting.

Second, insurers use reinsurance to help offset the reduction in PHS that otherwise can accompany writing too much business too fast.[42] By transferring all or a portion of the insurer's risk on specific policies or portfolios, an insurer increases its capacity to write additional new business. For example, insurers are typically required to maintain ratios of net written premium (NWP), i.e., the amount of premium an insurer writes less the amount ceded to reinsurers, to PHS of 3:1.[43] Through reinsurance, insurers can reduce net written premiums, increase surplus, and better manage NWP-to-PHS ratios within regulatory boundaries and within expectations of credit rating agencies.

Figure 2, based on a simplified scenario from the American Academy of Actuaries, illustrates this leveraging benefit:[44]

Insurer	Policyholders' Surplus (PHS)	Reinsurance	Net Written Premium (NWP)	Gross Written Premium (GWP)
ABC	$5 Million	None	$15 Million	$15 Million
XYZ	$5 Million	25% Quota Share on GWP	$15 Million	$20 Million

Figure 2. Quota Share Reinsurance Example.

In this example, both insurer ABC and XYZ have $5 million of PHS. Insurer ABC, which has not purchased reinsurance, has reached the maximum amount of premium ($15 million) that may be written based on its PHS of $5 million and the need to limit the NWP to PHS ratio to 3:1. In comparison, insurer XYZ is able to write an additional $5 million of gross premium while still maintaining the same 3:1 ratio, because of a reinsurance agreement. Under insurer XYZ's quota share reinsurance agreement, XYZ cedes 25 percent of its gross premiums (i.e., $5 million) and losses to a reinsurer. Insurer XYZ therefore may increase its market share while maintaining the specified NWP to PHS ratio.

Reinsurance offers related potential advantages for both parties to the contract. A cedent can maximize its use of sales, underwriting, policy administration and claims settlement capabilities, while limiting its risk for those underlying policies; correspondingly, the reinsurer(s) can absorb insurance risk exposures from the cedent and earn a share of profits from the underlying business without having to build distribution networks and underwriting and claims-handling infrastructures.[45]

3. Supporting Entry into and Exit from Insurance Markets

Reinsurance may assist insurers seeking to expand into new markets or to withdraw from particular segments. Even established insurers with ample capital may need support when entering new markets, new lines of business, or offering new products and features. Reinsurers can assist the transition by assuming a portion of the insurer's related risks. In addition, with regard to both new and established markets, reinsurers may offer advice and expertise on underwriting, pricing and claims-handling issues. Moreover, insurers sometimes wish to reduce or withdraw product offerings in particular markets. An insurer managing a discontinued line of business can transfer all or part of its related loss exposure to an assuming insurer through the use of reinsurance.

4. Promoting Capital Allocation Among Affiliates

Insurers are often owned by, or under common ownership and control with, other insurance companies. Separate insurance companies within a group may exist for legacy reasons (a result of past acquisitions), or might have been formed to operate in different jurisdictions for regulatory reasons, to sell different products, or to use different distribution systems.[46] Intraaffiliate reinsurance within a group may occur for many of the reasons that an insurer might otherwise purchase reinsurance from a non-affiliate. Additional reasons that are specific to the relationship between and among affiliates often include:

- *Pooling Arrangements* – Insurers that are part of a group may participate in a joint underwriting pool, in which the disparate underwriting experiences of participants are pooled together. The risks are then allocated back to one, some, or all participants sharing in that underwriting experience, each assuming through reinsurance its assigned portion of the aggregate underwriting results of the entire pool.
- *Efficient Capital Allocation* – Intra-company reinsurance can be used to tailor the risk or financial profile of separate legal entities within the group to address regulatory, rating agency, or managerial concerns. In addition, in some instances reinsurance through an affiliate may be more attractive, flexible or stable over time as compared with reinsurance available through the open market.
- *Reinsurance Captives in the U.S. Life Industry* – Life insurers sometimes use reinsurance on an intra-company basis to manage required statutory reserve levels. Regulatory concerns about this widespread practice continue to receive attention within the national and international insurance supervisory community.[47]

5. Achieving Risk Concentration or Diversification

Insurers generally seek a balance between risk concentration and diversification when underwriting one or more books of business. Insurers may use reinsurance to assist in achieving a targeted risk profile. While a large pool of relatively homogeneous risks may suit certain business objectives, including efficient use of a company's underwriting expertise, too much exposure to one class of risk might leave an insurer susceptible to adverse consequences due to that concentration (e.g., an accumulation of correlated exposures in a catastrophe-prone area). Risk transfer in this manner may be particularly important for smaller insurers that have more limited opportunities to diversify risk through underwriting practices than do larger insurers with risk profiles that include multiple lines of business written in multiple jurisdictions or across broader and more diverse geographic regions.[48]

B. The Importance of Reinsurance

The reinsurance marketplace is important to the U.S. insurance industry and, as such, contributes to the general economic prosperity of the country's families and businesses. As described above, reinsurance enhances the availability and affordability of insurance in the United States.[49] Available and affordable insurance helps spread risk, reduces financial uncertainty for businesses and individuals, provides private capital in a post-event recovery, and promotes economic growth. By spreading insurance risks globally, reinsurance diversifies local insurance markets while providing capital relief and balance sheet protection.

The extent to which U.S. property & casualty (P/C) insurers rely on reinsurance as of year-end 2013 is illustrated in Figure 3 on a line-by-line basis. The average utilization is approximately 19 percent across the board when considering both affiliated and unaffiliated reinsurers, and 12 percent taking only unaffiliated reinsurers into account. For property lines of insurance business, the average utilization is 18 percent for unaffiliated reinsurers, and is as high as 40 percent for allied lines.

Life insurers rely on domestic and international reinsurers to reduce losses, minimize exposure to significant risks, acquire or dispose of blocks of policies or business lines, and to provide additional capital for future growth. Ready access to diversified and well-capitalized reinsurance markets is important to maintain the financial strength of U.S. life insurers, to enable those insurers to meet policyholder obligations, and to expand access to affordable life insurance products in the United States.

In the property market, the key role of reinsurance may be most apparent following natural disasters and other catastrophes. Property catastrophe reinsurance provides a crucial backstop for insurers when low-frequency, high-severity events occur, and this market serves as an important illustration of the global nature of the reinsurance business. Catastrophe reinsurance indemnifies ceding insurers following an accumulation of insured losses from a single event, such as a hurricane, earthquake, tornado, winter storm, wild fire, or terrorist attack.[50]

Catastrophe protection as typically structured in reinsurance programs is comprised of a series of high-limit layers, often with multiple reinsurers participating to varying degrees on each layer. Catastrophe reinsurance programs are intended by the purchasing property insurers to provide reasonable assurance of protection for losses from one or more severe events in a given year (e.g., measured as a probable maximum loss for a 1-in-200 year event).

Line of Business	1	2	3	4	5	6			
	Direct Business	Reinsurance Assumed		Reinsurance Ceded		Net premiums Written Cols. 1 + 2 + 3 - 4 -5	Net Retention	Reins Utili- zation	Unafili- ated Reins Utili- zation
		From Affiliates	From Non- Affiliates	To Affiliates	To Non- Affiliates				
1 Fire	13,162,255,451	866,859,399	2,747,969,409	2,161,423,980	3,387,127,806	11,228,532,477	66.9%	33.1%	%
2 Allied lines	26,346,268,462	1,443,047,665	3,616,966,227	4,544,716,817	12,662,547,697	14,198,993,170	45.2%	54.8%	40.3%
3 Farmowners multiple peril	3,683,727,839	434,895,200	132,667,201	266,556,652	473,085,843	3,511,647,743	82.6%	17.4%	11.1%
4 Homeowners multiple peril	80,671,706,514	149,856,374	2,746,363,323	1,392,825,252	9,402,771,084	72,772,333,520	87.1%	12.9%	11.3%
5 Commercial multiple peril	37,933,389,810	818,556,543	1,820,735,846	2,639,970,124	4,688,006,032	33,244,702,411	81.9%	18.1%	11.6%
6 Mortgage guaranty	4,549,732,713	13,662,445	27,717,048	20,988,352	240,177,288	4,329,946,572	94.3%	5.7%	5.2%
8 Ocean marine	3,955,929,531	124,095,252	751,729,484	259,613,133	1,708,630,958	2,863,510,172	59.3%	40.7%	35.4%
9 Inland marine	17,256,885,852	429,588,043	462,459,220	1,378,839,149	6,623,103,682	10,146,990,290	55.9%	44.1%	36.5%
10 Financial guaranty	674,864,316	80,186,749	12,931,202	(4,430,339)	61,931,125	710,481,483	92.5%	7.5%	8.1%
11.1 Medical professional liability - occurrence	2,408,868,965	(36,593,085)	109,374,131	45,755,078	146,306,113	2,289,588,821	92.3%	7.7%	5.9%
11.2 Medical professional liability - claims-made	7,363,251,622	57,861,693	373,010,765	763,858,820	780,163,729	6,250,101,239	80.2%	19.8%	10.0%
12 Earthquake	2,292,589,227	35,401,429	316,486,513	523,017,593	534,468,045	1,586,991,523	60.0%	40.0%	20.2%
13 Group accident and health	4,688,655,561	587,435,340	947,149,060	338,329,910	1,178,713,053	4,706,196,993	75.6%	24.4%	18.9%
14 Credit accident and health (group and individual)	208,639,731	60,627,832	2,082,912	35,791,338	169,796,126	65,763,010	24.2%	75.8%	62.6%
15 Other accident and health	1,771,736,150	407,833,898	694,186,408	(26,073,129)	132,987,487	2,766,821,265	96.3%	3.7%	4.6%

Line of Business	1	2	3	4	5	6			
	Direct Business	Reinsurance Assumed		Reinsurance Ceded		Net premiums Written Cols. 1 + 2 + 3 - 4 -5	Net Retention	Reins Utili-zation	Unafili-ated Reins Utili-zation
16 Workers' compensation	49,312,678,773	359,674,597	2,106,409,617	4,524,024,181	6,116,390,281	41,138,348,528	79.5%	20.5%	11.8%
17.1 Other liability - occurrence	33,878,793,848	1,317,670,979	4,173,260,401	5,455,896,423	7,152,714,565	26,761,114,244	68.0%	32.0%	18.2%
17.2 Other liability - claims-made	19,598,774,816	304,008,990	1,966,796,523	3,481,645,018	3,093,822,540	15,294,112,776	69.9%	30.1%	14.1%
17.3 Excess Workers' Compensation	1,070,757,369	2,737,487	89,061,503	169,147,726	149,309,393	844,099,242	72.6%	27.4%	12.8%
18.1 Products liability - occurrence	2,885,306,864	45,652,155	111,053,942	438,822,348	295,532,101	2,307,658,510	75.9%	24.1%	9.7%
18.2 Products liability - claims-made	560,201,527	23,134,676	43,745,077	82,266,208	133,594,984	411,220,091	65.6%	34.4%	21.3%
19.1, 19.2 Private passenger auto liability	111,134,418,384	616,948,097	2,259,531,921	1,923,419,790	4,640,706,278	107,446,772,336	94.2%	5.8%	4.1%
19.3, 19.4 Commercial auto liability	20,505,362,474	529,227,294	1,076,924,773	2,012,165,151	1,745,516,744	18,353,832,664	83.0%	17.0%	7.9%
21 Auto physical damage	76,893,751,207	238,032,716	1,334,199,254	3,341,180,979	2,135,861,928	72,988,940,282	93.0%	7.0%	2.7%
22 Aircraft (all perils)	1,731,716,771	104,795,354	384,284,140	349,325,315	803,748,320	1,067,722,628	48.1%	51.9%	36.2%
23 Fidelity	1,203,151,960	53,027,559	70,897,871	51,232,623	151,645,850	1,124,198,921	84.7%	15.3%	11.4%
24 Surety	5,255,473,663	334,076,363	494,314,120	729,977,396	483,147,632	4,870,739,113	80.1%	19.9%	7.9%
26 Burglary and theft	233,695,811	7,728,892	14,312,957	31,818,715	18,665,967	205,252,983	80.3%	19.7%	7.3%
27 Boiler and machinery	1,558,937,570	116,251,535	1,230,367,283	229,221,927	696,815,371	1,979,519,083	68.1%	31.9%	24.0%
28 Credit	1,881,380,055	113,347,106	262,587,874	595,533,564	494,460,735	1,167,320,742	51.7%	48.3%	21.9%
29 International	76,365,530	8,475,954	80,189,703	39,206,894	12,651,382	113,172,907	68.6%	31.4%	7.7%
30 Warranty	2,518,589,527	6,607,878	42,704,051	615,825,806	796,735,751	1,155,339,900	45.0%	55.0%	31.0%

(Continued)

Line of Business	1	2	3	4	5	6			
	Direct Business	Reinsurance Assumed		Reinsurance Ceded		Net premiums Written Cols. 1 + 2 + 3 - 4 -5	Net Retention	Reins Utili-zation	Unafili-ated Reins Utili-zation
31 Reinsurance - Nonproportional Assumed Property	XXX	704,548,183	9,840,701,005	2,108,680,923	724,312,181	7,712,256,083			
32 Reinsurance - Nonproportional Assumed Liability	XXX	115,942,435	6,233,917,019	1,597,034,052	181,992,366	4,570,833,032			
33 einsurance - Nonproportional Assumed Financial Lines	XXX	25,092,957	205,336,625	38,638,381	5,527,352	186,263,844			
34 Aggregate write-ins for other lines of business	1,378,557,731	3,062,845	38,832,725	176,092,236	112,299,414	1,132,061,650	79.7%	20.3%	7.9%
35 TOTALS	538,646,415,616	10,503,358,830	46,821,257,145	42,332,338,387	72,135,267,197	481,503,380,221	80.8%	19.2%	12.1%
Casualty Lines	378,403,731,878	5,685,297,470	18,711,864,617	23,652,050,455	40,361,891,751	338,786,930,672	84.1%	15.9%	10.0%
Property Lines	144,159,491,513	3,371,569,685	10,918,285,701	12,926,807,173	28,633,445,172	116,889,069,887	73.8%	26.2%	18.1%
Financial Lines	16,083,192,234	600,908,100	911,152,166	2,009,127,402	2,228,098,381	13,358,026,731	75.9%	24.1%	12.7%

Source: ANNUAL STATEMENT for the year December 31, 2013 of the P/C Combined Industry.

Figure 3. P/C Reinsurance Utilization By Line of Insurance.

The United States is a large insurance market, with a high degree of private market insurance penetration, and insurers writing U.S. business have substantial exposure to catastrophe losses. Seven of the ten costliest catastrophes in the world, as measured by insured losses, occurred in whole or in part in the United States.[51] Hurricanes Katrina, Rita, and Wilma in 2005 resulted in about $90 billion of U.S. insured property losses, of which non-U.S. reinsurers paid approximately $59 billion.[52]

Likewise, reinsurers indemnified insurers for about 60% of the insured losses from the September 11th terrorist attacks, which at the time was the largest insured loss in U.S. history.[53] More recently, Superstorm Sandy in 2012 resulted in an estimated $26 billion of insured losses, with insurers accounting for approximately $19 billion of this amount.[54] Approximately 40 percent of the loss to insurers was reimbursed through reinsurance.[55]

Of course, it is not only in the United States that consumers, businesses and insurers are subject to the risk of loss from catastrophes. Recent decades have been described as a new era for catastrophes world-wide.[56] Global insured catastrophe losses reached $116 billion in 2011, which was the second worst catastrophe year as measured by insured loss. Reinsurers assumed more than half of those insured catastrophe losses.[57]

As Figure 4 illustrates, while the number of events has declined from the 2005 peak, the global trend has been toward increasing numbers of catastrophes. When viewed in recent historical context (particularly with respect to Atlantic hurricanes affecting the U.S.), relatively few natural catastrophes occurred in 2013. Nonetheless, the U.S. experienced nine significant natural catastrophes (winter storms, thunderstorms with tornado outbreaks, and flooding), each exceeding $1 billion in economic loss. The aggregate natural disaster loss of nearly $13 billion in 2013 was substantially below the average of the preceding 10 years. Globally, 2013 saw more than $3.5 billion of losses in Germany from hailstorms, $3 billion of losses in central Europe from flooding, and over $1.5 billion of losses in Canada from flooding. Typhoon Haiyan caused thousands of deaths and devastating property loss in the Philippines. Worldwide insured natural catastrophe losses in 2013 were approximately $31 billion.[58]

Moreover, while individuals, businesses, governments, and insurers have a shared interest in implementing mitigation measures, the need for risk transfer mechanisms to address exposure to catastrophic losses will likely continue to increase. Several studies have shown, for example, that many natural disasters which occurred in the past (and which are capable of repetition) would be far more costly were they to occur today, and that in general loss severity from natural catastrophes will continue to grow.[59]

International reinsurers are of particular importance to the U.S. insurance industry following catastrophes, when insurance capital plays an essential role in post-event recovery. Reinsurers support the insurers that contribute billions for reconstruction efforts and which aid property owners and local, state and regional economies.[60]

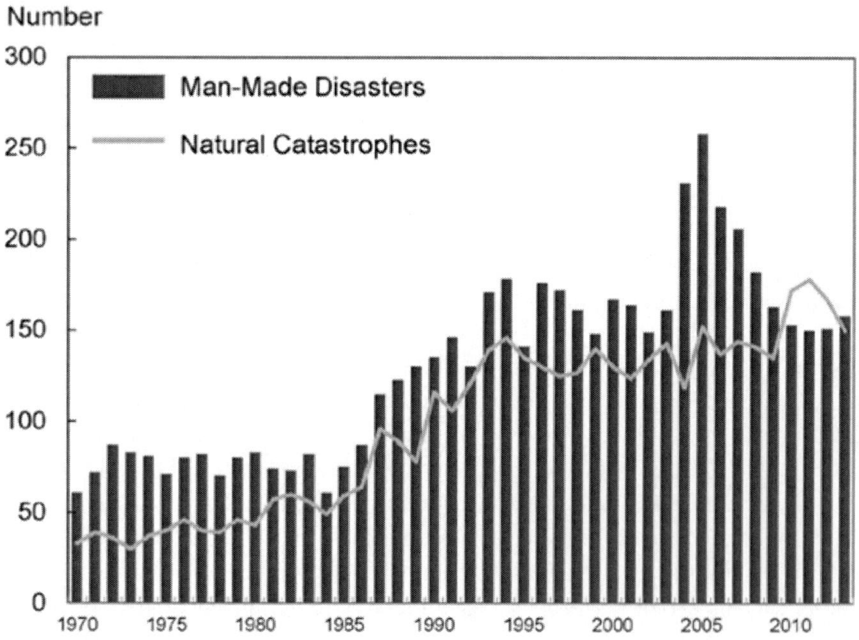

Source: Swiss Re, sigma No 01/2014, Natural Catastrophes and Man-made Disasters in 2013 (2014).

Figure 4. Number of Events -- 1970-2013.

V. Regulation of Reinsurance in the United States

Although the business of insurance is primarily regulated at the state level, the U.S. insurance sector is in a larger sense subject to an integrated federal-state framework.[61] A state insurance regulator focuses on the financial strength (solvency) of the insurers that are subject to the jurisdiction of that regulator, as well as on market conduct issues (e.g., product design, pricing, and claims payment practices). Among other interstate and international prudential matters relating to insurance, the federal government is involved with oversight of savings and loan holding companies that control insurers, as well as any insurer that may be a nonbank financial company that the Financial Stability Oversight Council (Council) determines should be subject to supervision by the Board of Governors of the Federal Reserve System and enhanced prudential standards.[62]

While reinsurance serves a range of important functions, regulators recognize that it can concentrate credit risk into comparatively few counterparties. The credit risk created by reinsurance—which often involves large transactions—can be measured by the amount of reserves a reinsurer holds for losses, loss adjustment expenses and life, annuity and health insurance benefits.[63] These reserves are based on the expected future claims payments on the risks assumed from the ceding insurers. Such credit risk is mitigated because the transactions must be conducted according to a prudential regulatory framework that limits the amount of risk that is transferred to any one reinsurer,[64] requires the use of collateral in certain cases, and requires appropriate amounts of capital to be held by the ceding insurers.

Regulation of the business of reinsurance in the U.S. is considered to be either direct or indirect. Inasmuch as reinsurance is part of the business of insurance, it is directly regulated primarily at the state level in the United States if the reinsurer is licensed or domiciled in a given state.

As described below, a substantial portion of reinsurance supporting the U.S. insurance sector is provided by companies not licensed in all states and, in many cases, neither domiciled nor licensed in the United States. While a non-U.S. company may establish one or more reinsurance affiliates in the U.S., developing that corporate structure would require each insurance subsidiary to be licensed in each relevant state, which may limit the flow of capital. A company reinsuring U.S. cedents that is not "authorized"[65] by any state would not be subject to direct regulation by state insurance regulators, but that company nonetheless is indirectly regulated through requirements under state laws on the cedent-licensees and by certain terms of reinsurance contracts.

A. Direct Regulation

In the United States, a state insurance regulator directly regulates reinsurers domiciled and licensed in its state as well as reinsurers licensed in its state but domiciled in another state.[66] When an insurer cedes business to a licensed reinsurer, the cedent is permitted under regulatory accounting rules to recognize a reduction in its liabilities for the amount of ceded liabilities, without a regulatory requirement for the reinsurer to post collateral to secure the reinsurer's ultimate payment of the reinsured liabilities. A reinsurer licensed in a state is subject to solvency and other regulations imposed by the state which are applicable to insurance companies generally.[67] Each state, for example, specifies a minimum level of capital and surplus that licensed insurers and reinsurers must maintain. State laws also address restrictions or limits on an insurer's investment portfolios, impose risk-based capital requirements, and provide for on-site examinations, annual and quarterly statement filings, and actuarially-certified opinions, among other requirements.[68]

B. Indirect Regulation

A large and increasing proportion of reinsurance premiums from U.S.-based insurers are ceded to reinsurers based outside the United States that are not licensed by any U.S. state, and thus not directly subject to prudential regulation by any state.[69] While state insurance regulators do not have direct supervisory authority over such non-state licensed non-U.S. reinsurers, longstanding state laws pertaining to the terms and conditions of reinsurance contracts to which U.S. cedents are party amount to indirect reinsurance regulation of those cedents' reinsurers. Such laws impose limitations on the ability of a licensed U.S. insurer to receive "credit for reinsurance" in its regulatory financial statement unless certain obligations by the reinsurer are met. For the reasons outlined above in section IV.A, an insurer's ability to take credit for the reinsurance is an important aspect of the transaction; therefore, as a practical matter the imposition of such regulatory requirements on the cedent and on the form of the reinsurance contract becomes a business requirement that the cedent must, in turn, impose on its unlicensed reinsurers.

A key requirement has been (and generally remains) that in order to receive financial statement credit for unauthorized reinsurance, a U.S. cedent must be the beneficiary of security posted by the reinsurer, providing collateral equal to 100 percent of the actuarially-estimated liabilities under the reinsurance contract.[70]

In 2011, state insurance regulators unanimously approved amendments to the NAIC's Model Law which, if enacted into law or otherwise implemented in a state, would authorize that state's insurance regulator to certify certain unauthorized reinsurers for reduced collateral requirements. As of October 2014, some form of authorization for the state insurance regulator to accept less than 100 percent collateral from non-U.S. reinsurers had been adopted in 23 states, but those state laws and regulations have not necessarily been uniform in structure or implementation. FIO has stated previously that uniformity should be pursued with respect to the supervision of reinsurance, including collateral requirements, because global diversification and capital allocation are beneficial to the U.S. insurance industry and the consumers that rely on it.[71] The subjects of reinsurance collateral reform and the role of the federal government in establishing such uniformity are addressed in section V.D of this Report.

C. Federal Involvement in Reinsurance and Industry Oversight

The federal government participates in multiple reinsurance programs for markets served by private market insurers or reinsurers, including: (1) the Federal Crop Insurance Corporation (FCIC),[72] under which the federal government provides reinsurance to commercial writers of crop insurance; (2) the Price-Anderson Nuclear Industries Indemnification Act,[73] under which nuclear power licensees are required to contribute to a fund (currently limited to approximately $13 billion) in the event of an incident leading to damages exceeding coverage under commercial insurance policies;[74] (3) the Overseas Private Investment Corporation (OPIC),[75] an independent government corporation providing political risk insurance to support investment by U.S. businesses in emerging markets and developing countries, and which may use reinsurance in fulfilling its mandate; (4) the aviation war risk program,[76] under which the Federal Aviation Administration (FAA) supplies insurance or reinsurance for aircraft when the President determines that commercial air service is necessary in the interest of national defense or foreign policy, and the Secretary of the U.S. Department of Transportation determines that such insurance could not be obtained on reasonable terms in the private market; and (5) the National Flood Insurance Program (NFIP), under which the federal government (through the Federal Emergency Management Agency, FEMA) sells residential flood insurance, and which under recent legislation may in the future be supported by private market reinsurance.[77]

In addition, the Terrorism Risk Insurance Act (TRIA), a post-September 11, 2001, law establishing the Terrorism Risk Insurance Program (TRIP) in Treasury, provides a backstop for insured commercial property and casualty losses resulting from a certified "act of terrorism."[78] As of publication of this Report, TRIA will expire on December 31, 2014. Terrorism risk insurance supports a broad range of economic activities across the United States, and in some instances may be prohibitively expensive or unavailable in the absence of TRIP.[79]

Treasury also has a longstanding regulatory role with respect to reinsurers of companies writing surety bonds for federal projects.[80] Treasury's Surety Bond Branch certifies insurers to directly write and reinsure federal surety bonds. A "surety bond" is a contract under which one party (the surety) guarantees the performance of certain obligations of a second party (the principal) to a third party (the obligee). By regulation, sureties can cover excess risks on federal surety bonds through reinsurance provided by Treasury-certified reinsurers. Treasury also approves "admitted reinsurers," which Treasury-certified sureties can use to cover non-Federal excess risks.

Several provisions of the Dodd-Frank Act have implications regarding federal roles in the oversight of reinsurance. First, Part II of the Nonadmitted and Reinsurance Reform Act of 2010 (NRRA) specifically addresses the regulation of reinsurance.[81] The purpose of the NRRA is to enhance uniformity in the state-based solvency regulation of insurers and reinsurers by increasing deference to the state in which the reinsurer is domiciled or licensed.

The NRRA addresses this goal by designating the regulator from a reinsurer's domiciliary state as the sole state regulator responsible for the financial solvency of the reinsurer.[82] Previously, each state in which a reinsurer was licensed had the authority to regulate the reinsurer, which could make the reinsurer subject to as many as 56 state-law standards. In addition, the NRRA provides that if an insurer is domiciled in an NAIC-accredited state,[83] and that state has allowed the insurer to take financial statement credit for certain reinsurance, then another state may not deny the insurer such credit for reinsurance.[84] Previously any state could, and certain states did, impose disparate extraterritorial regulatory regimes addressing credit for the same reinsurance.[85]

Second, the Director of FIO is a member of the Council and is authorized to recommend that the Council designate a nonbank financial company that is an insurer (or an affiliate of an insurer) to be subject to supervision by the

Federal Reserve and enhanced prudential standards.[86] Nonbank financial companies that could be subject to these authorities may include reinsurers.[87]

Finally, the Dodd-Frank Act authorizes FIO to "coordinate federal efforts and develop federal policy on prudential aspects of international insurance matters, including representing the United States, as appropriate, in the International Association of Insurance Supervisors [IAIS]."[88] Currently, the Director of FIO serves as a member of the IAIS Executive Committee as well as Chair of its Technical Committee. The Technical Committee is developing the Common Framework (ComFrame) for the Supervision of Internationally Active Insurance Groups (IAIGs).[89] The criteria for supervisory identification of an IAIG would apply to IAIGs that are reinsurers as well as to those that are primary insurers.[90]

In the international context, the IAIS is involved in the development of global capital standards for the insurance sector as called upon by the Financial Stability Board (FSB).[91] In 2014, the IAIS published a Basic Capital Requirement (BCR) applicable to a global systemically important insurer (G-SII).[92] The BCR is intended to serve as a foundation for Higher Loss Absorbency (HLA) requirements, an additional capital component that would apply to G-SIIs, and which remains in development. The IAIS is also developing a more comprehensive and risk-sensitive Insurance Capital Standard (ICS) which would be applicable to IAIGs (which includes G-SIIs). It is presently anticipated that from 2019, the ICS will commence to apply to IAIGs, and could then replace the BCR as the foundation for HLA requirements. International insurance standards are not self-executing, and are without legal effect in the United States until implemented through a federal or state process.[93]

FIO's Director is also one of six members of the Steering Committee of the EU-U.S. Insurance Project (the Project), the objective of which is to contribute to an increased mutual understanding and enhanced cooperation between the EU and the United States in order to promote business opportunities, consumer protection and effective insurance supervision.[94] Significant components of the Project focus on the regulation of collateral for reinsurance and on examining differences between such regulation in the EU and the United States. The Project – which includes representation of a range of European and domestic stakeholders (including U.S. state regulators) – has also been exploring how to achieve a consistent approach within each jurisdiction, including consideration of reductions and possible removal of collateral requirements in both jurisdictions in favor of a risk-based determination for all reinsurers in relation to a cedent's credit for reinsurance.

With regard to reinsurance, the *Modernization Report* recommends development of a uniform and transparent solvency oversight regime for the transfer of risk to reinsurance captives, and pursuit of a covered agreement for reinsurance collateral requirements.[95] A covered agreement is a written bilateral or multilateral agreement between the United States and one or more foreign governments, authorities, or regulatory entities regarding prudential measures with respect to the business of insurance or reinsurance which meets certain specified standards.[96] Work towards initiating negotiations for a covered agreement with leading reinsurance jurisdictions continues.[97]

D. Credit for Reinsurance Collateral Reform

As discussed above, regulatory oversight of the reinsurance industry in the United States is part of the integrated federal-state framework applicable to the insurance sector generally. Non-U.S. reinsurers accepting reinsurance premium ceded from U.S. insurers, however, are not subject to the same state-based prudential supervision applicable to licensed or accredited U.S. insurers and reinsurers. Rather, non-U.S. reinsurers are supervised by the regulatory regime of the applicable overseas jurisdiction. Such reinsurers, when doing business with U.S. cedents, have for many years been "indirectly" regulated by state laws requiring that in order for cedents to obtain "credit for reinsurance" the non-U.S. reinsurer must post 100 percent collateral for all reinsurance liabilities assumed from that cedent. Such "credit for reinsurance laws," which exist in every state, are based on the Credit for Reinsurance Model Act and Regulation ("Model Law") of the NAIC, dating to 1984.

Reform efforts — which would consider the efficacy of regulatory supervision in non-U.S. jurisdictions by permitting less than 100 percent collateral — have been under consideration by the NAIC and various states since at least 2001.[98] In December of 2005, the Ad Hoc Reinsurance Collateralization Roundtable (formed in 2004 and consisting of nine U.S. insurance regulators) presented a report to the NAIC Reinsurance Task Force expressing "substantial agreement" that a system for varying the amount of collateral required from unauthorized reinsurers according to financial strength and reliability was feasible.[99] In 2006, the NAIC Reinsurance Task Force published a white paper providing a "balanced synopsis of the historical arguments in favor of and against amending U.S. reinsurance collateral requirements," in order to provide that task force with a basis for making further public policy recommendations on the issue.[100]

In 2008, Florida became the first state to introduce reduced collateral requirements for some unauthorized reinsurance, followed in 2011 by New York, Indiana and New Jersey, with collateral reform adopted in those states by April 2011. The scope and details of these reforms differ in multiple respects, but all permit collateral reduction for some reinsurers accepting business ceded from licensed insurers.

In November 2011, the NAIC adopted – through the unanimous approval of state insurance regulators – amendments to the Model Law that would permit state regulators discretion to designate "certified reinsurers" domiciled in countries determined by the NAIC to be "qualifying jurisdictions."[101] Certified reinsurers would be eligible for reduced regulatory collateral standards, based on the nature and strength of the regulatory regime in the reinsurer's home jurisdiction and on individualized objective and subjective analysis, including considerations of financial strength, credit rating, and reputation.[102] The Model Law is not self-executing and does not create law in any state. Whether, when, and in what form amendments to the Model Law become a law or regulation is a matter for the respective states.[103]

FIO is authorized to coordinate federal efforts and develop federal policy on prudential aspects of international insurance matters. In this role, FIO's *Modernization Report* calls for reform to afford "nationally uniform treatment of reinsurers with respect to collateral requirements." 104 The *Modernization Report* states Treasury's concerns regarding implementation of the amended Model Law, including:

- A determination by one state within the United States of the adequacy or the equivalence of regulation by another nation would not bind other states, possibly resulting in frustration of broader U.S. economic or regulatory policy.
- The amended Model Law depends too heavily upon assessments of a reinsurer's creditworthiness by credit rating agencies. A preferable approach would be for other risk-based, empirical factors to be the basis upon which to determine the creditworthiness of the reinsurer.
- Nineteen additional states[105] have now adopted some form of collateral reform based on the amended Model Law; among those states, however, authorization to accept less than 100 percent collateral has not been uniform in the structure or implementation of the state law requirements.

Non-U.S. reinsurers argue that collateral requirements restrict the ability to manage risk globally, restrict reinsurance capacity in the United States, and thus increase costs for U.S. consumers. Non-U.S. reinsurers account for 62 percent or more of reinsurance premiums ceded by U.S.-based insurers.[106] Moreover, EU authorities have recently adopted "Solvency II"—a modernized insurance regulatory regime which goes into effect in January 2016 and which calls for evaluation of regulatory treatment of reinsurers in non-EU jurisdictions. Risk-based regulation of reinsurance collateral requirements will improve opportunities for U.S. reinsurers operating in the EU.

In formulating federal policy on prudential aspects of international insurance matters, federal officials are well-positioned to make determinations regarding whether a foreign jurisdiction has sufficiently effective regulation and, in doing so, consider other prudential issues pending in the United States and between the United States and affected foreign jurisdictions.[107] Accordingly, Treasury, together with the United States Trade Representative (USTR), is considering whether to include collateral requirements.[108] The covered agreement could have the effect of preempting inconsistent state laws.[109]

VI. Global Reinsurance Markets

A. The U.S. Insurance Sector as Purchasers of Reinsurance

By premium volume, the United States is the largest single-country insurance market in the world, and the business of insurance is a substantial component of the U.S. economy. Domestic insurers directly employ approximately 2.3 million people.[110] In 2013, U.S. insurers wrote approximately $1.3 trillion in total premiums.[111] The U.S. insurance sector reported $5 trillion in total assets in 2013.[112]

Broadly viewed, the two principal sectors of the U.S. primary insurance market are:

- The Property & Casualty (P/C) Sector. This sector refers generally to insurance products offering protection to policyholders for financial loss associated with damage to physical property as well as loss from legal liability. The P/C sector in the United States is comprised of more than 2,700 insurers of varying size, specialization and geographic diversity,[113] offering products broadly categorized as either personal lines (e.g., homeowners or automobile insurance) or commercial lines (e.g., workers' compensation, professional liability, or commercial multi-peril insurance)—each of which accounts for approximately half of 2013 P/C premiums. In 2013, P/C aggregate direct premiums were approximately $544 billion.[114]

- The Life & Health (L/H) Sector. This sector refers generally to insurance coverage for losses associated with accidents, death, long-term care, or disability. The sector also includes annuity products that create a revenue stream for policyholders (e.g., for retirement planning) in addition to providing death benefits. The L/H sector in the United States is comprised of approximately 1,000 insurers,[115] and in 2013, L/H sector aggregate direct premiums totaled approximately $750 billion.[116] Of this, approximately $570 billion arose from life business (including annuity products) and $180 billion from A/H business.[117]

As further described below, U.S. insurers in both of these sectors rely on U.S. and non-U.S. reinsurers. Measured by total ceded premium, the United States is the largest single-country reinsurance market in the world. Roughly half of all reinsurance business originates from North America.[118]

As a commercial activity, reinsurance is usually purchased and sold in private market transactions. Through various state and federal programs, however, public entities are or may be parties to reinsurance transactions (Box 2).

Box 2: Examples of Government Programs Associated with Purchasing or Supplying Reinsurance

The Florida Hurricane Catastrophe Fund (FHCF) is a government-owned reinsurance entity, created in 1993 after Hurricane Andrew in order to "protect and advance the state's interest in maintaining insurance capacity in Florida by providing reimbursements to insurers for a portion of their catastrophic hurricane losses."[119] The FHCF is structured as a tax-exempt trust fund, operated by an agency of the Florida government (State Board of Administration of Florida), and provides a backstop to insurers of non-commercial property in Florida.[120] The FHCF is partially funded through collected premiums, and relies in part on tax-exempt, post-event revenue bonds for shortfalls and recapitalization. The bonds are funded by assessments on most lines of P/C insurance.[121]

The California Earthquake Authority (CEA) was established following the 1994 Northridge earthquake to address severe reductions in availability of earthquake insurance.[122] The CEA operates as a publicly managed, privately financed, regulated insurance entity, offering earthquake insurance for California residential property. Coverage is not subsidized, and is distributed by private insurers that choose to participate in the CEA; funding capital is provided by participating insurers, which also retain a specified degree of exposure. The CEA purchases reinsurance in the commercial marketplace, including through capital markets.[123]

The National Flood Insurance Program (NFIP) is a federal program administered by the Federal Emergency Management Agency (FEMA),[124] which makes flood insurance (some at subsidized rates) available for qualified property. Pursuant to the Biggert-Waters Flood Insurance Reform Act of 2012 – which extended the program for five years – the NFIP is authorized to "secure reinsurance of coverage provided by the flood insurance program from the private market at rates and on terms determined by the Administrator to be reasonable and *appropriate, in an amount sufficient to maintain the ability of the program to pay claims.*"[125]

Other market participants involved in the purchase of reinsurance include reinsurance brokers, also known as intermediaries. Reinsurance brokers are licensed by the individual states and provide a range of services to insurers, such as assistance in designing and placing reinsurance programs as well as offering reinsurance billing and claims services. Reinsurance brokers may also provide technical expertise to insurers such as catastrophe modeling and enterprise risk management advice. Although some "direct" reinsurers conduct business with cedents without using any intermediary, the use of brokers who can access worldwide reinsurance markets is common.

B. Global Suppliers of Reinsurance

The reinsurance industry operates on a cross-border basis from jurisdictions throughout the world. The transnational nature of the business of reinsurance serves to diversify exposure to risk. Referring to the 2005 hurricane season, which included three major storms causing losses in the United States, an IAIS report explained:

> Reinsurers contribute to the global diversification of risks and to an efficient allocation of capital and improved risk management on the side of primary insurers.... Without access to global reinsurance capacity the claims burden arising from this exceptional sequence of natural catastrophes would have fallen on U.S. domestic (re)insurers and U.S. subsidiaries of non-U.S. parents. The access to global reinsurance and the reinsurance recoveries obtained from global and domestic reinsurance by primary insurers mitigated the financial impact these catastrophes would have had on U.S. primary insurers and by extension also on U.S. policyholders.[126]

This section provides a range of comparative industry data demonstrating the breadth and global scope of the reinsurance industry. First, this section presents data addressing various economic metrics for the reinsurance industry. It then provides industry data on a geographic basis – starting with the U.S. reinsurance industry and then turning to non-U.S. reinsurance markets which support U.S. insurers. A single, standardized source of data regarding the international reinsurance industry does not currently exist. This report relies primarily on data published by A.M. Best and Standard & Poor's (credit rating agencies that provide annual and periodic updates on the global insurance and reinsurance industries); Aon Benfield and Guy Carpenter (global insurance and reinsurance brokers); Swiss Re, Munich Re, the Reinsurance Association of America, and the IAIS.

1. Reinsurance Industry Data

Data regarding the global reinsurance industry both illustrate its breadth and scope and demonstrate its importance to the U.S. insurance industry.

For example, Figure 5 show the top reinsurance groups, constituting the bulk of the global reinsurance market, as compiled by A.M. Best As illustrated in Figure 5, the top five global reinsurers account for more than $120 billion of gross premiums written in 2013 (with Munich Re and Swiss Re accounting for $71 billion of that figure), with the next 45 largest reinsurance groups combined to write approximately $103 billion of gross premium.

Figure 6 shows the countries and regions most involved in the geographically diffuse reinsurance industry. Over 27 percent of worldwide reinsurance premiums are written (assumed) by German companies. The London market (including Lloyd's) represents nearly 9 percent of the market, and the rest of Europe accounts for about 10 percent. Bermuda and the Asian Pacific regions each represent approximately 11 percent of assumed business, while Switzerland and the Americas (United States, Canada, and Latin

America) each assume approximately 15.5 percent. As displayed in Figure 7, if only reinsurance of non-life business is considered, the global distribution is somewhat different, with the Americas only writing approximately 10 percent of worldwide premiums, and Bermuda markets writing roughly 15.5 percent. Both Figure 6 and Figure 7 are based on the domicile of the reinsurers' ultimate parent company.

2014 Ranking	Company	Gross Written Premium Life & Non-Life	Gross Written Premium Non-Life Only	Total Shareholders' Funds
1	Munich Reinsurance Company	38,333	23,423	36,108
2	Swiss Re Ltd.	32,934	20,670	32,977
3	Hannover Rueckversicherung AG	19,225	10,764	8,991
4	Lloyd's	15,614	15,594	33.619
5	SCOR S.E.	14,116	6,675	6,856
6	Berkshire Hathaway Inc.	12,776	7,339	224,485
7	Reinsurance Group of America Inc.	8,573	0	5,936
8	China Reinsurance (Group) Corporation	7,936	4,947	7,512
9	Korean Reinsurance Company	5,623	4,995	1,381
10	PartnerRe Ltd.	5,562	4,590	6,766
11	Everest Re Group Ltd.	5,219	5,219	6,968
12	Great West Lifeco	4,206	0	18.701
13	Transatlantic Holdings, Inc	3,423	3,423	4,486
14	MAPFRE RE, Compania de Reaseguros S.A.	2,524	2,102	1,390
15	General Insurance Corporation of India	2,377	2,356	5,243
16	The Toa Reinsurance Company, Limited	2,269	2,269	1,523
17	XL Group plc	2,218	1,894	11,349
18	Assicurazioni Generali SpA	2,178	930	29,470
19	QBE Insurance Group Limited	2,155	2,155	10,403
20	Axis Capital Holdings Limited	2,138	2,138	5,868
21	R+V Versicherung AG	2,095	2,058	2,632
22	Odyssey Re Holdings Corp.	1,868	1,868	3,731
23	Catlin Group Limited	1,850	1,850	3,783
24	Caisse Centrale de Reassurance	1,750	1,611	2,719
25	Amlin plc	1,701	1,701	2,768
26	RenaissanceRe Holdings Ltd.	1,605	1,605	3,904
27	Arch Capital Group Ltd.	1,489	1,489	5,648
28	MS&AD Insurance Group Holdings, Inc.	1,417	1,417	21.725
29	Validus Holdings, Ltd.	1,390	1,390	4,202
30	Deutsche Rueckversicherung AG	1,369	1,320	279
31	IRB - Brasil Resseguros S.A.	1,308	1,255	1,066
32	Endurance Specialty Holdings, Ltd.	1,190	1,190	2,887
33	Aspen Insurance Holdings Limited	1,134	1,134	3,300
34	Markel Corporation	1,134	1,133	6,678
35	White Mountains Insurance Group, Ltd.	1,120	1,120	4,397
36	ACE Limited	1,057	1,057	28,825
37	American Agricultural Insurance Company	941	941	489
38	Allied World Assurance Company Holdings, AG	934	934	3,520
39	Tokio Marine Holdings, Inc.	923	923	26,033
40	Pacific LifeCorp	896	0	8,970
41	Maiden Holdings, Ltd.	868	868	1.124
42	W.R. Berkley Corporation	809	809	4,369
43	ACR Capital Holdings Pte, Ltd.	797	797	700
44	NKSJ Holdings, Inc.	726	726	13,212
45	Montpelier Re Holdings Ltd.	706	706	1,887
46	African Reinsurance Corporation	670	635	678
47	Platinum Underwriters Holdings Ltd.	580	580	1,747
48	Greenlight Capital Re. Ltd.	536	536	1.086
49	Central Reinsurance Corporation	522	321	487
50	Wilton Re Holdings Limited	506	0	1,357

Source: A.M. Best, Global Reinsurance – Segment Review (September 2014).

Figure 5. Top 50 Global Reinsurance Groups (GWP $ millions).

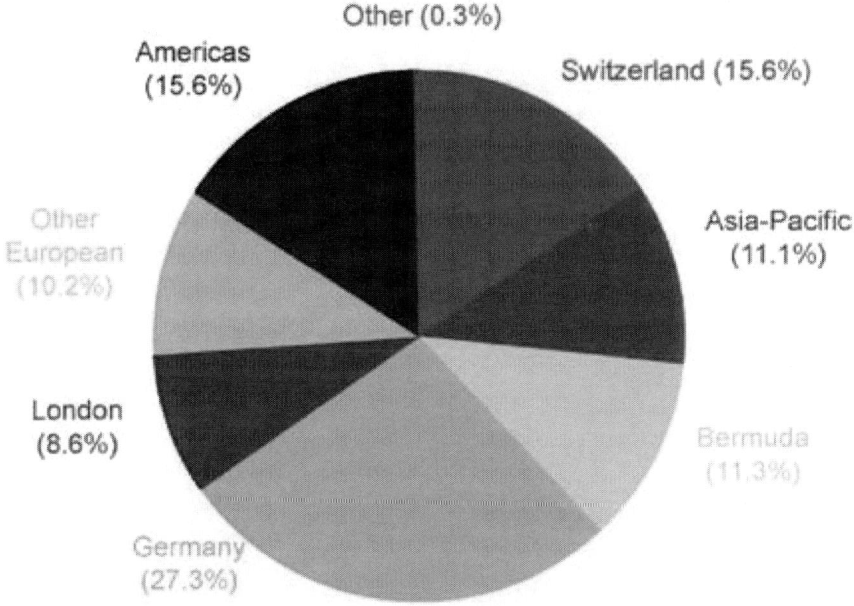

Source: A.M. Best, Global Reinsurance – Segment Review (September 2014)

Note: Region determined by ultimate parent's domicile. Americas includes U.S., Canada and Latin America. Americas GPW includes Berkshire Hathaway subsidiaries National Indemnity and General Re Corp.

Figure 6. Global Reinsurance – Gross Premiums Written by Region (2013).

As displayed in Figure 7, if only reinsurance of non-life business is considered, the global distribution is somewhat different, with the Americas only writing approximately 10 percent of worldwide premiums, and Bermuda markets writing roughly 15.5 percent. Both Figure 6 and Figure 7 are based on the domicile of the reinsurers' ultimate parent company.

One way to view the global nature of the reinsurance industry is to consider the relative transfer of risk between geographic regions. Analysis by the IAIS shows that European insurers and reinsurers are "net insurance risk takers," i.e., these entities assumed $47 billion more in reinsurance premium than ceded. In contrast, North American entities ceded $16 billion more reinsurance premium than assumed. These data, which demonstrate that reinsurers are geographically diverse from the reinsured risks, are displayed in Figure 8.

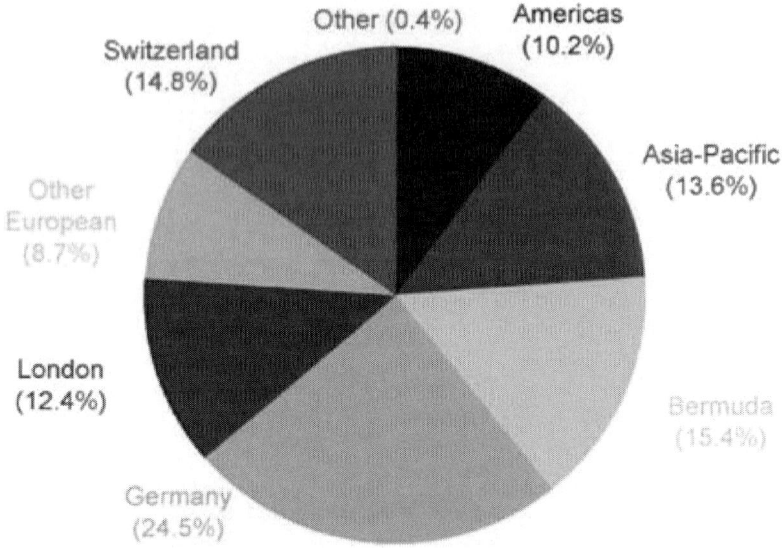

Source: A.M. Best, Global Reinsurance – Segment Review (September 2014)

Note: Region determined by ultimate parent's domicile. Americas includes U.S., Canada and Latin America. Americas GPW includes Berkshire Hathaway subsidiaries National Indemnity and General Re Corp.

Figure 7. Global Reinsurance – Non-Life Gross Premiums Written by Region (2013).

Company	(1) Gross Assumed by Reporting Entities	(2) Gross Ceded to Reporting Entities	Net Position (1-2)
Europe	$99	-$52	$47
North America	$72	-$88	-$16
Asia and Australia	$2	-$23	-$21
Africa and Middle East	-	-$4	-$4
Latin American	-	-$7	-$7

Source: International Association of Insurance Supervisors, Global Insurance Market Report, 20 (2012) (referencing 2011 data).

Figure 8. Risk Transfer Between Regions ($ Billions).

The global diversity of reinsurance is not limited to the geographic domicile of reinsurers; as Figure 9 illustrates, global reinsurance premiums are widely distributed across sectoral lines of business. Property exposures represent the largest share, driven in part by property insurers' demand for catastrophe protection.[127]

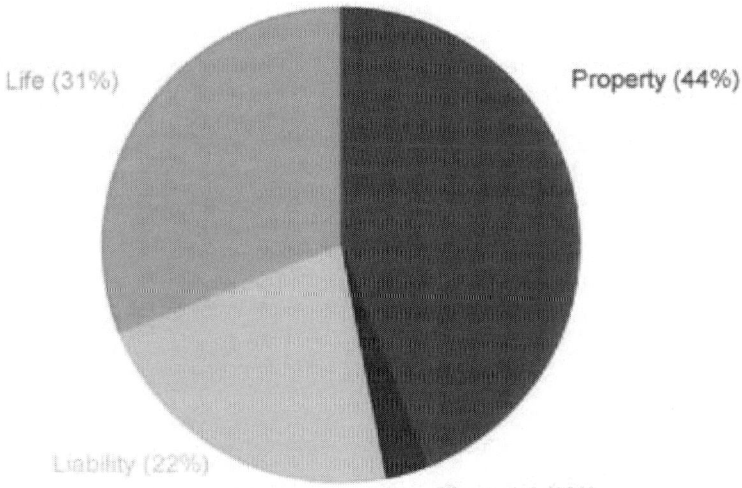

Source: International Association of Insurance Supervisors, Global Insurance Market Report (2012) (referencing 2011 data).

Figure 9. Global Reinsurance Premiums by Sectoral Line of Business.

Dedicated reinsurance capital and reinsurance premiums written by the top reinsurers and largest reinsurance groups show yet another perspective of the global scope of the reinsurance industry. The IAIS has noted that the combined assets of the ten largest reinsurers – which together constitute roughly 90 percent of the global L/H market and 50 percent of the non-life market – are less than the assets of the single top primary insurer. By market capitalization, the entirety of the reinsurance industry approximates that of the two top primary insurers.[128] Similarly, as displayed in Figure 10, the IAIS estimates that worldwide reinsurance premiums (approximately $200 billion in all) are two percent of primary life premiums and about nine percent of primary non-life premiums; retrocessional premiums (reinsurers' purchase of further reinsurance), in turn, are about $25 billion.[129]

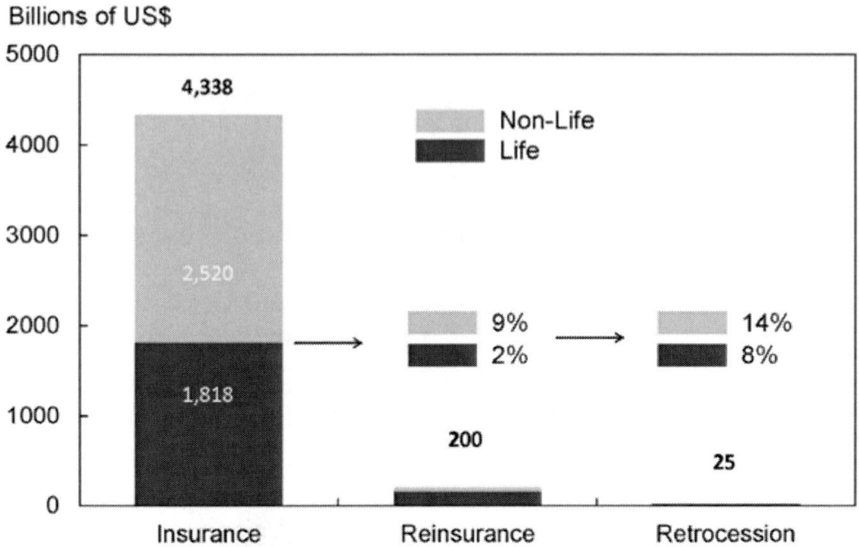

Source: International Association of Insurance Supervisors, Reinsurance and Financial Stability, 9 (2012) (referencing 2010 data).

Figure 10. Global Premium Volume ($ Billions).

For a variety of reasons relating in part to the timing and manner in which such data are reported and published in various jurisdictions, estimates of total capital within the reinsurance industry vary substantially among sources. In a calculation that provides "a broad measure of capital available for insurers to trade risk with and includes both traditional and alternative forms of reinsurance capital," Aon Benfield reports that total global reinsurance capital in 2013 approximated $540 billion, a figure that includes $50 billion in alternative capital (such as catastrophe bonds).[130]

Global reinsurance capitalization is at record levels, a development that has been accompanied by softening of reinsurance premium rates.[131] For example, for catastrophe reinsurance, global renewal premiums fell 11 percent year-over-year at January 2014,[132] and for U.S. catastrophe risks, the year-over-year premium reduction was 15 percent. The trend continued with respect to reinsurance that renewed in April 2014,[133] June 2014, and July 2014,[134] and likely will continue into 2015.[135] In addition to a period of below-average catastrophe losses,[136] market capacity expansion, including the increased importance of alternative reinsurance options (addressed below in section VI.C) and accompanying competition for deployment of reinsurance capital partially explain this trend of decreasing reinsurance premiums.[137] Analysts have suggested that some industry consolidation might occur due to the sector's current competitive climate.[138] Over the course of 2014, all of the major rating agencies announced negative outlooks for the reinsurance industry.[139]

2. United States Reinsurance Sector

In 2013, the P/C reinsurance market in the United States consisted of about 26 U.S.-based reinsurers operating either as individual companies or groups, five of which accounted for more than half of the $29.1 billion of net written (assumed) premium.[140] Some of the leading reinsurers in the United States (included in the foregoing data) are affiliates of groups headquartered overseas. For example, QBE North America is an affiliate of QBE Insurance Group Limited (Australia), and Munich Reinsurance America is an affiliate of Munich Re Group (Germany). The combined surplus for these 26 reinsurers was $146.2 billion as of year-end 2013 and $128 billion for 2012.[141] In 2013, $96.3 billion of that surplus was attributable to asingle company, National Indemnity Company, which is a subsidiary of Berkshire Hathaway, Inc.[142]

In recent years the share of premium ceded by U.S. insurers to non-U.S. reinsurers has been increasing steadily. As seen in Figure 11, the share of premiums ceded by U.S. insurers to U.S.- based reinsurers declined fairly uniformly from 61 percent in 1997 to only 38 percent in 2013.[143]

When the countries of the reinsurers' ultimate parent companies are taken into consideration, the importance of the global reinsurance market to U.S. ceding companies is even more evident. Reinsurers owned by groups headquartered or domiciled outside the United States accounted for approximately 92 percent of reinsurance premiums ceded by U.S.-based insurers in 2013.[144] Other than U.S. subsidiaries of offshore companies, a new U.S.-domiciled reinsurer has not been formed in over two decades.[145]

The U.S. life reinsurance market is led by a relatively few global reinsurers. In October 2013, SCOR SE, a French-based reinsurance group, completed its acquisition of Generali's U.S. life reinsurance operations, giving SCOR SE the largest share of life reinsurance business in the United States.[146] Other major participants assuming U.S. life reinsurance business include Reinsurance Group of America, Inc. (RGA), Swiss Reinsurance Co. Ltd., and Munich Reinsurance Co. In 2012, these reinsurers comprised 83 percent of the life reinsurance market for U.S. risks.[147] Of the four, RGA is the only life reinsurer primarily headquartered at the group level in the United States.

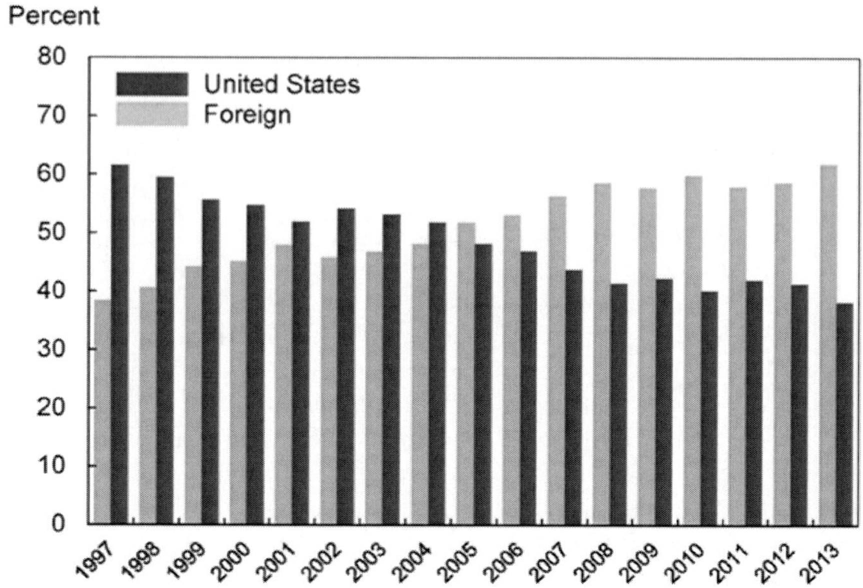

Source: Reinsurance Association of America, Offshore Reinsurance in the U.S. Market: 2013 Data (2014).

Figure 11. Market Share of U.S. and Non-U.S. Reinsurers (U.S. Cessions).

In sum, non-U.S. reinsurers play an integral role in the U.S. insurance market. Today, non-U.S. and foreign-controlled companies assume the majority of premiums ceded by U.S. insurers.

3. Non-U.S. Reinsurance Sector

With more than 200 companies offering reinsurance throughout the world,[148] the global reinsurance market is robust and provides important support to U.S. insurers. Of the $28.4 billion in U.S. premiums ceded to non-U.S. companies in 2013, most were assumed by reinsurers in seven jurisdictions: Bermuda ($9.7 billion), United Kingdom ($4.8 billion), Germany ($3.7 billion), Cayman Islands ($3.3 billion), Switzerland ($1.4 billion), Channel Islands ($1.3 billion), and Turks & Caicos ($1.0 billion).[149]

a. Europe

Five of the six largest reinsurance groups in the world, by premium volume, are based in Europe: Munich Reinsurance Co., Swiss Reinsurance Co.

Ltd., Hannover Rueckversicherung AG, SCOR SE and the Lloyd's market. The combined net L/H and P/C premiums written by these reinsurers were approximately $107 billion on a group basis in 2013.[150] The largest reinsurance jurisdictions within Europe, by net reinsurance premiums written and the domicile of the individual legal entity reinsurer, are Germany ($52.3billion), United Kingdom ($13.5 billion), Switzerland ($15.5 billion), Ireland ($8.6 billion), and France ($7.9 billion).[151]

b. Bermuda

Unlike the European reinsurance market, which has existed for more than a century, the development and expansion of the Bermuda reinsurance industry is more recent. Bermuda did not experience noticeable growth in the traditional reinsurance market until the late 20th century.[152] Since then, Bermuda has emerged as an important domicile for reinsurers, with a substantial concentration of capital and reinsurance-related resources. A recent industry report noted: "Among other things, Bermuda offers relatively quick regulatory approval to launch operations (a few weeks), favorable tax laws (zero corporate income tax), and proximity to the U.S., the largest reinsurance market in the world (650 miles off the coast of North Carolina)."[153]

The growth of the Bermuda reinsurance market has reflected the cyclical nature of the overall reinsurance market. Bermuda has attracted new market entrants during cycles when worldwide reinsurance capital was low and prices for reinsurance had increased. In 1992, for example, a number of new reinsurers were organized in Bermuda to take advantage of high demand and favorable reinsurance prices following Florida's devastating Hurricane Andrew. Additional growth spurts, which occurred in waves following major loss-making disasters, have accentuated an overall upward trend in the number of new reinsurers and reinsurance affiliates in Bermuda throughout the last two decades.

According to the Standard & Poor's analysis of 2013 data, Bermuda hosts 15 of the world's largest reinsurance groups, as measured by net reinsurance premiums, including two in the top ten (PartnerRe Ltd. and Everest Reinsurance Co.).[154] As of 2013, Bermuda-based reinsurers held approximately 8 percent of the global reinsurance market, doubling the share from 4 percent a decade earlier.[155] Gross premiums written by Bermuda reinsurers reached $76 billion in 2013; a third of this business is property (including property catastrophe).[156] The bulk of Bermuda insurance and reinsurance premiums (roughly half of GWP) are generated from North American risks.[157]

c. Asia-Pacific

Although not as large as European reinsurance groups, Asia-Pacific reinsurers are nonetheless key participants in the international arena. Seven of the world's largest reinsurance groups are based in the Asia-Pacific region.[158] In 2013 these reinsurers combined to assume almost $19 billion in net written premiums. The Asia-Pacific reinsurance market is largely driven by reinsurers domiciled in Japan ($10.89 billion), Korea ($3.57 billion), India ($2.21 billion), and Australia ($1.77 billion).[159]

Despite significant losses following the 2011 catastrophes, including the Tohoku earthquake and tsunami in Japan and the Christchurch earthquake in New Zealand, Asia-Pacific reinsurers largely replenished capital and maintained strong credit ratings.[160] Asia-Pacific reinsurers likely will continue to seek risk in the United States and other areas of the world to complement and diversify risk portfolios, particularly in light of various regional factors currently presenting challenges to the industry (e.g., consolidation of regional insurers and slowing growth rates in developing markets).[161]

d. Increasing Capital Markets Convergence with Reinsurance

The reinsurance market typically operates through the traditional structure in which one or more reinsurers assume a portion of an insurer's risk in return for a specified premium. In recent years, however, managers of hedge funds, pension funds, and other equity funds (collectively referred to herein as "capital markets") have increasingly looked to the reinsurance market as a means of diversifying portfolios, capitalizing on cyclical trends in reinsurance pricing, and improving investment yield.

Capital markets may be attracted to the reinsurance business partly because of the low correlation between investment risk and underwriting risk. Underwriting results of reinsurers generally do not track the investment returns of broader financial markets—the influence of natural disasters on the value of equity markets, corporate bonds, and other financial investments, for example, is uncorrelated to the effect of such events on insurers.[162]

Alternative reinsurance solutions may be employed to protect cedents against a variety of risks, but these instruments have primarily been geared toward property catastrophe risks, which offer a relatively short time horizon to maturity, allowing investors to participate in contracts of a few years or less and evaluate returns soon after contract expiration.[163] Furthermore, alternative reinsurance augments existing traditional property catastrophe reinsurance capacity, which typically requires dedication of a large amount of capital during a short period. Property catastrophe models have developed to a point where capital markets are able to assess the levels of assumed natural disaster risk with sufficient reliability.[164]

The nature of investors comprising this capital market is varied. One report states that over half of the capital supporting alternative reinsurance originates from "pension funds, endowments and sovereign wealth funds, generally through specialized insurance-linked investment funds."[165]

Over a quarter of the capital comes from hedge funds and private equity funds, while about 10 percent emanates from reinsurers looking for an alternative avenue to obtain returns.[166]

1. Types of Alternative Reinsurance

Alternative reinsurance instruments take a number of forms, including those described below.

- *Catastrophe (Cat) Bond* – A cat bond is a structured debt instrument that transfers risk from a sponsor (i.e., an insurer) to investors (i.e., the capital markets) under terms and conditions similar to a reinsurance contract.[167] To create a cat bond, an insurer establishes a special purpose vehicle (SPV) that issues notes to investors. The notes contain conditions similar to a reinsurance contract, so that default on the bond would result under circumstances which would be loss-making under a typical reinsurance catastrophe contract.[168] Funds raised by investors are managed by the SPV in a segregated collateral account which is available to pay the sponsoring company in the event of a loss. If an event does not occur, the premium paid to the SPV by the sponsor, the principal on the note, and investment income earned thereon are returned to the investors.[169] A cat bond's trigger may take various forms, such as an indemnity trigger (i.e., the actual incurred loss of the sponsor), a parametric trigger (i.e., a description of the physical characteristics of the catastrophe), or an industry loss trigger (i.e., the amount of insured loss incurred by the industry).[170] Of these, an indemnity trigger is now by far the most common.
- *Sidecar* – A sidecar is a temporary reinsurance vehicle that shares premiums and losses exclusively with an insurer primarily on a pro-rata basis, generally for business associated with catastrophe risk. Formation of a sidecar involves a number of different parties. A sponsor, either an insurer or, in the case of a retrocession, a reinsurer,

will establish a company (the sidecar) for a limited purpose and duration.[171] The sidecar may be financed by debt and equity through third party investors (i.e., capital markets). The proceeds from the debt, equity, and premiums ceded by the sponsor are placed in a trust account as collateral for losses that may arise under ceded insurance policies.[172]

- *Industry Loss Warranty (ILW)* – An ILW is a contract that provides coverage for an insurer if the industry-wide insurance loss from an event satisfies a pre-determined condition.[173] The insurer's own loss will usually also be required to trigger payment under an ILW contract.
- *Collateralized Reinsurance* – Collateralized reinsurance is a fully collateralized insurance-linked security that can be tailored to supplement the terms and conditions of a traditional reinsurance contract. The collateral, posted by investors, is equal to the coverage limits of the reinsurance net of the premium. The collateral is held in a separate account to satisfy losses due to the ceding insurer; the reinsurance premiums constitute the investor's return.[174]
- Similar to traditional reinsurance solutions, alternative reinsurance instruments offer a variety of benefits to cedents (and retrocedents), such as providing an element of diversification to an insurer's reinsurance portfolio. In addition, the collateralization of a cat bond helps reduce credit risk and enhances predictability of reinsurance costs since the bond terms typically last several years.[175] A sidecar may be used to provide an additional source of reinsurance to an insurer when the reinsurance market has limited capital (e.g., following a natural disaster) and therefore allows an insurer to write more business during a time when rates are high.[176] An ILW offers low transaction costs because the payout is linked to an industry loss figure, not the specific portfolio of an insurer; and thus an ILW may offer a more affordable solution to catastrophe protection.[177] Collateralized reinsurance allows non-traditional reinsurers to efficiently offer additional capacity for catastrophe loss, often on a retrocession basis.[178]

2. Development of the Alternative Reinsurance Market

The alternative reinsurance market gained popularity during the 2000s when insurers (and reinsurers) sought additional ways to protect against increasing losses from catastrophes. During a time when equity markets and other reinsurers were infusing capital into new unaffiliated and affiliated reinsurance companies, insurers were also looking to alternative reinsurance instruments as an additional avenue for capacity and diversification. This sector has continued to expand, even as market capacity has increased and rates have declined.[179] One industry analyst recently noted: "Reinsurers will continue to incorporate the competitive strengths of alternative capital flows into their capital and organizations through (i) sponsorship of catastrophe bonds to lower their cost of underwriting capital supporting tail risks; (ii) sponsorship of sidecars to lower their cost of underwriting capital throughout their underwriting risk distribution; and (iii) formation of insurance-linked securities and collateralized reinsurance fund management units."[180]

In the wake of the September 11th attacks, the total amount of cat bonds outstanding in 2002 was $2.9 billion. Hurricanes Katrina, Rita, and Wilma in 2005 brought further interest in alternative products. By 2008, the total amount of cat bonds outstanding had reached $16 billion.[181] Sidecar reinsurance capacity has also grown over time, from just over $1 billion in the period between 1999 and 2001 to over $7 billion in the period between 2005 and 2007.[182] In 2009, nontraditional reinsurance collectively was about $20 billion in total capacity.[183] More recently, growth in this segment has been driven by "investors ... looking for better-than-average returns in the short term," rather than insurers seeking solutions for post-catastrophe capacity issues.[184]

In recent years, the non-traditional reinsurance market has continued to evolve, and it is now a standard consideration for many reinsurance buyers. Broker Guy Carpenter estimates a total of $20.5 billion in cat bonds outstanding as of mid-2014 (Figure 12). In the first quarter of 2014, sponsors issued $1.6 billion of insurance-linked securities, primarily cat bonds, which was a record amount for a single quarter.[185] The second-quarter set another new record, with the issuance of $4.6 billion in cat bonds.[186] Insurance-linked securities investments for calendar year 2014 are on track to set a new annual record.[187]

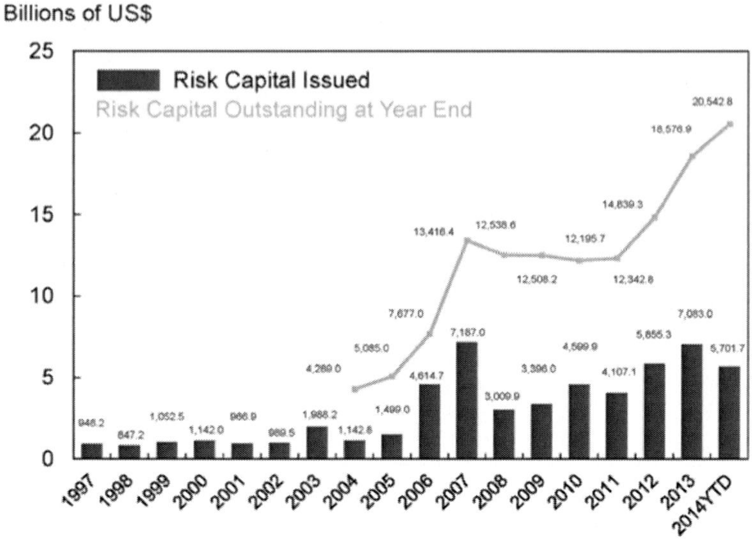

Source: Guy Carpenter, Capital Markets: The Reinsurance Evolution Continues (September 2014).

Figure 12. Growth of Cat Bonds.

Although cat bonds and other P/C insurance financing vehicles are the most common form of insurance-linked securities, life insurers have also participated in this market. Prior to the financial crisis, life insurers used interest-linked securities mainly to manage statutory capital and reserve requirements. Principal and interest obligations on these securities were often guaranteed by a single financial guarantor. During the crisis, some of those guarantors encountered credit problems, resulting in lower use of interest-linked securities by life insurers post-crisis. More recently, several insurers and reinsurers have sponsored the issuance of excess mortality bonds,[188] while others have used alternative markets to transfer longevity risk or monetize expected emergence of profits on defined blocks of business.[189]

The growth of alternative risk transfer markets extends interconnections between the insurance and reinsurance sector and capital markets. While such instruments serve the economic function of expanding markets for catastrophe and other insurance risks, exposure to such risks could be problematic for unsophisticated investors. These instruments have been described as increasingly mainstream products,[190] although the long-term commitment of non-traditional capital sources has not yet been tested. As some analysts have noted, very few cat bonds to date have experienced major losses.[191]

CONCLUSION

The strength and viability of both the insurance and reinsurance sectors are vitally important to the United States, which is the largest single-country insurance market in the world. As authorized under the Dodd-Frank Act, FIO monitors the insurance industry and has produced this Report regarding "the breadth and scope of the global reinsurance market and the critical role such market plays in supporting insurance in the United States."[192]

While this Report does not analyze the extent to which reinsurance or any particular reinsurer could be systemically important, the business of reinsurance is global in scope, and serves multiple important purposes within the U.S. insurance sector. The global reinsurance market provides access to the financial strength of reinsurers and to alternative risk transfer capital, thereby assisting insurers in preparing for and responding to catastrophes and natural disasters. In addition, reinsurers assist insurers in stabilizing underwriting experience, increasing underwriting capacity, and facilitating entrance to and exit from markets, thereby helping insurers maintain product pricing that is more available and affordable, which benefits the U.S. economy as a whole. Reinsurers also promote capital allocation among affiliates and address risk diversification. In light of the importance of the global reinsurance market to U.S. insurers, and for other reasons described in this Report, Treasury and USTR are considering a covered agreement with respect to collateral requirements for reinsurers.

The majority of unaffiliated reinsurance purchased by U.S. insurers is obtained from non-U.S. reinsurers. The traditional reinsurance market is now supplemented with capital from alternative sources, which has created a growing range of risk transfer sources for insurance companies, such as catastrophe bonds and collateralized reinsurance. As this Report describes, the global reinsurance market provides an essential backstop and various risk and capital management mechanisms for insurance in the United States.

End Notes

[1] International Association of Insurance Supervisors, Reinsurance and Financial Stability, 19 (July 19, 2012).

[2] Dodd-Frank Act §§ 501-502, 31 U.S.C. § 313 (2010).

[3] See, e.g., 31 U.S. § 313(c)(1)(A).

[4] 31 U.S.C. § 313(o)(1).

[5] All comments available at http://www.treasury.gov/initiatives/fio/reports-and-notices/Pages /closed.aspx.

[6] The combined assets of the ten largest reinsurers – which together constitute roughly 90% of the global life and health reinsurance market and 50% of the non-life reinsurance market – are smaller than the assets of the top insurer, and by market capitalization the whole reinsurance sector equals the two top primary insurers. International Association of Insurance Supervisors, Reinsurance and Financial Stability (July 19, 2012).

[7] Henry T. Kramer, The Nature of Reinsurance, in Reinsurance (Robert W. Strain, ed. 1980) at 8. David M. Holland, A Brief History of Reinsurance, Reinsurance News (Society of Actuaries), Issue 65, 19 (February 2009).

[8] David M. Holland, A Brief History of Reinsurance, Reinsurance News (Society of Actuaries), Issue 65, 10-14 (February 2009).

[9] Id. (citing Samuel Marshall, A Treatise on the Law of Insurance in Four Books, Second American from the second London edition, U. S. cases collected by J. W. Condy, Vol. I & II (Philadelphia: William P. Farrand and Co., 1810), p. 18)).

[10] Henry T. Kramer, The Nature of Reinsurance, in Reinsurance (Robert W. Strain, ed. 1980) at 8 (referencing the market at Lloyd's of London).

[11] Id. at 15.

[12] See, e.g., Mutual Safety Ins. Co. v. Hone, 2 N.Y. 235 (1849).

[13] David M. Holland, A Brief History of Reinsurance, Reinsurance News (Society of Actuaries), Issue 65, 22-23 (February 2009).

[14] Id. (noting that ten new U.S. reinsurers were formed between 1910 and 1920).

[15] Id. at 19.

[16] See generally Comment in response to the FRN on behalf of Lloyd's, 1, 3 (August 27, 2012); About Us: The Lloyds' Market, available at http://www.lloyds.com/lloyds/about-us/what-is-lloyds/the-lloyds-market.

[17] David M. Holland, A Brief History of Reinsurance, Reinsurance News (Society of Actuaries), Issue 65, 23 (February 2009).

[18] History of Mendes & Mount LLP (noting that as counsel to Lloyd's, "the Firm helped set up a fund of cash reserves to be used in case of a crippling financial disaster in England as the result of war"), available at http://www.mendes.com/firm/.

[19] See generally Lloyd's United States Trust Deeds, available at http://www.lloyds.com/the-market/operating-atlloyds/regulation/lloyds-trust-deeds/united-states-trust-deeds.

[20] National Association of Insurance Commissioners, U.S. Reinsurance Collateral White Paper, 20 (March 5, 2006).

[21] See section V.D of this Report.

[22] Insurance Act 1978 (as amended), Consolidated Laws of Bermuda.

[23] "After large catastrophes, which tend to reduce global capacity and lead to temporary rate increases in certain lines of business, the [reinsurance] market has traditionally seen an inflow of start-up companies. ... On balance, these dynamics kept the non-life reinsurance market comparatively competitive." International Association of Insurance Supervisors, Reinsurance and Financial Stability, 16 (July 19, 2012). "Reinsurance markets are inherently cyclical." Standard & Poor's Ratings Services, Global Reinsurance Highlights 2014, 21 (2014).

[24] J. David Cummins, The Bermuda Insurance Market: An Economic Analysis, 11 (May 6, 2008). In each instance, roughly eight to eleven new reinsurers were established in Bermuda.

[25] Standard & Poor's tracks 40 "Global Reinsurers." See Standard & Poor's Ratings Services, Global Reinsurance Highlights 2014: Innovation and Adaption are Key to Relevance (2014). A.M. Best regularly addresses the "Top 50 Global Reinsurance Groups." See A.M. Best, Global Reinsurance – Segment Review: The Capital Challenge - How Relevant is the Underwriting Cycle (September 2014).

[26] Reinsurance Association of America, Offshore Reinsurance in the U.S. Market: 2013 Data, 4, 13 (2014). The data are approximate, based on analysis of U.S. insurer annual reports, and disregard reinsurance between affiliated companies.

[27] See section VI.C of this Report.

[28] The dips in 2008 and 2011 correspond to Hurricanes Ike and Irene, respectively, and reflect the cyclical nature which has characterized the global reinsurance market. See Part VI of this Report.

[29] Reinsurance Association of America, Fundamentals of P/C Reinsurance, available at http://www.reinsurance.org/Fundamentals.

[30] Glossary, in Reinsurance Contract Wording (Robert Strain, ed. 1992), 755. This differs from some direct (or "primary") insurance policies, which are more commonly contracts of "liability" rather than of indemnity. See generally Skandia America Reins. Corp. v. Schenk, 441 F. Supp. 715, 724 (S.D.N.Y. 1977). Exceptions to this general practice include (1) certain instances, for example in the case of a catastrophe, in which a reinsurer might advance a payment to an insurer with the understanding that the insurer's payment to policyholders is inevitable; and (2) in case of insolvency of an insurer, in which state regulators require that the obligations of the reinsurer to the estate of the insolvent insurer is not diminished because of the inability of the insurer to pay its direct obligation to policyholders in whole or in part. To address the latter situation, state insurance regulations require an "insolvency clause" as a standard term in reinsurance contracts. In addition, some reinsurance contracts and alternative risk transfer instruments incorporate "parametric" or industry loss triggers, calling for payment based upon the occurrence of a specified industry loss amount or an agreed index.

[31] Comment in response to the FRN on behalf of Reinsurance Association of America, 2 (August 27, 2012).

[32] Morris & Co. v. Skandinavia Ins. Co., 279 U.S. 405, 408 (1929); Citizens Cas. Co. v. Am. Glass. Co., 166 F.2d 91, 95 (7th Cir. 1948).

[33] David M. Raim and Joy L. Langford, Understanding Reinsurance, in New Appleman on Insurance Law Practice Guide, § 40.01 (2007).

[34] Comment in response to the FRN on behalf of Association of Bermuda Insurers and Reinsurers, 13 (August 27, 2012). Reinsurers generally keep proportionately more risk "net" as compared to primary insurers. According to the IAIS, retrocessional premiums amounted to $25 billion worldwide in 2012. International Association of Insurance Supervisors, Reinsurance and Financial Stability, 9 (July 19, 2012).

[35] The reinsurer typically has rights, however, to review and audit the cedent's portfolio of insurance policies subject to the treaty in order to satisfy itself that the ceded business is of the type which the reinsurer agreed to cover.

[36] Henry T. Kramer, "The Nature of Reinsurance," in Reinsurance (Robert W. Strain, ed. 1980) at 9-11. "Utmost good faith," while not generally regarded in law as rising to the level of a fiduciary relationship, characterizes a relationship in which "the maxim of caveat emptor has no application to either party." Id. at 9.

[37] See section IV.A.3 of this Report.

[38] The ceding commission compensates the cedent for producing and administering the ceded business. The surplus relief function may be particularly important for life insurers due to the relatively high acquisition costs.

[39] "Retention," the amount of loss the cedent keeps for its own account, is a reinsurance term roughly analogous to a deductible under an insurance policy. Glossary, in Reinsurance Contract Wording (Robert Strain, ed. 1992), 767.

[40] David M. Raim and Joy L. Langford, Understanding Reinsurance, in New Appleman on Insurance Practice Guide, § 40.04[1] (2007). For example, the particular insured risk may be excluded under the relevant treaty, or the ceding insurer's exposure may fall within the treaty's retention.

[41] Retrocession provides many of the same benefits to a retrocedent as reinsurance provides to a primary insurer (e.g., allowing the retrocedent to write more business and providing risk diversification).

[42] Policy acquisition costs, such as agents' and brokers' commissions, are expensed when paid at the inception of the policy for regulatory accounting purposes, rather than deferred as an asset and amortized over the term of the respective policies.

[43] Comment in response to the FRN on behalf of American Academy of Actuaries, 2 (August 27, 2012).

[44] This simplified example excludes reference to ceding commission and other expenses associated with reinsurance transactions, as well as changes in surplus.

[45] Comment in response to the FRN on behalf of Insurance Law Committee of NYC Bar Association, 4 (August 24, 2012).

[46] Id.

[47] See Department of the Treasury, Federal Insurance Office Annual Report on the Insurance Industry (2014), 43-44 (hereinafter FIO 2014 Annual Report) (addressing progress of states in reforming regulatory oversight respecting transfer of risk to life captives); Department of the Treasury, How to Modernize and Improve the System of Insurance Regulation in the United States, 32 (December 2013) (hereinafter Modernization Report) (recommending that states develop a uniform and transparent solvency oversight regime for the transfer of risk to reinsurance captives). Both reports available at http://www.treasury.gov/ initiatives/fio/ reports-and-notices/.

[48] International Association of Insurance Supervisors, Reinsurance and Financial Stability, 7 (July 19, 2012); Comment in response to the FRN on behalf of Insurance Europe, 2 (August 27, 2012).

[49] See Swiss Re, The Essential Guide to Reinsurance, 14-22 (2013); Comment in response to the FRN on behalf of Reinsurance Association of America, 14 (August 27, 2012).

[50] Since shortly after the September 11, 2001, terrorist attacks, the federal government has provided a backstop for certain insured losses resulting from terrorism through the Terrorism Insurance Program ("TRIP"), pursuant to the Terrorism Risk Insurance Act of 2002, 15 U.S.C. § 6701 note. See The President's Working Group on Financial Markets, The Long-Term Availability and Affordability of Insurance for Terrorism Risk (2014). TRIP is scheduled to expire on December 31, 2014.

[51] Munich Re, Significant Natural Catastrophes 1980 – 2013, available at http://www.munichre.com/site/corporate/get/documents_E-1423023189/mr/assetpool.shared/Documents/5_Touch/_NatCatService/Significant-Natural-Catastrophes/2013/10-costliest-events-ordered-by-insured-losses-worldwide.pdf.

[52] Comment in response to the FRN on behalf of Insurance Europe, 3 (August 27, 2012).

[53] Comment in response to the FRN on behalf of Association of Bermuda Insurers and Reinsurers, 5 (August 27, 2012).

[54] Insurance Journal, 1 Year After Superstorm Sandy: Quick Economic Facts (October 2013), available at http://www.insurancejournal.com/news/east/2013/10/29/309538.htm (additionally, approximately $8 billion in losses were paid by the National Flood Insurance Program).

[55] Global Reinsurance Forum, Global Reinsurance: Strengthening Disaster Risk Resilience, 11 (September 2014).

[56] Kunreuther, H. and Michel-Kerjan, E., At War with the Weather: Managing Large-Scale Risks in a New Era of Catastrophes, Preface, MIT Press (2009).

[57] Swiss Re, sigma No 01/2013, Natural Catastrophes and Man-made Disasters in 2012, 2 (2013).

[58] See generally Munich Re, 2013 Natural Catastrophe Year In Review (Jan. 7, 2014), available at http://www.iii.org/assets/docs/pdf/MunichRe-010714.pdf.

[59] See, e.g., Swiss Re, U.S. Tornadoes: An Examination of the Past to Prepare for the Future – Modeling for a Complex and Growing Peril (2014), available at http://media.swissre.com/documents/2014_us_tornadoes.pdf (observing that the primary drivers of increased tornado loss severity are population growth, asset growth, and value growth); Karen Clark & Co, Historical Hurricanes that Would Cause $10 Billion or More of Insured Losses Today (August 2012), available at http://www.karenclarkandco.com/pdf/HistoricalHurricanes_Brochure.pdf; (identifying 28 historical storms which, if occurring today with the same meteorological parameters, would likely cause $10 billion or more of insured losses); Swiss Re, The Big One: The East Coast's USD 100 Billion Hurricane Event (September 2014), available at http://media.swissre.com/documents/the_big_one_us_hurricane.pdf (modeling the 1821 Norfolk and Long Island hurricane).

[60] See, e.g., International Association of Insurance Supervisors, Reinsurance and Financial Stability, 8 (July 19, 2012).

[61] In 1945, Congress enacted the McCarran-Ferguson Act to clarify that state laws governing the business of insurance are not invalidated, impaired, or superseded by any federal law unless the federal law specifically relates to the business of insurance. 15 U.S.C. §§ 1011-1015. Section II of the Modernization Report discusses the history of insurance regulation in the United States, including an explanation of how the current state-based system developed.

[62] See generally section V.C below.

[63] At the end of 2013, for example, U.S. P/C reinsurers reported $63 billion in loss and loss adjustment expense reserves. Reinsurance Association of America, Offshore Reinsurance in the U.S. Market: 2013 Data, 10 (2014). By contrast, overall insurance industry P/C reserves were nearly $600 billion. FIO 2014 Annual Report, 26.

[64] See, e.g., 11 CRR-NY § 125, et seq. (New York regulations); 18 Del. Code. § 911 (Delaware regulations).

[65] An "authorized" insurer is one that is licensed or accredited in a given state. See generally Kimberly M. Welsh, Regulation of Reinsurance, in New Appleman on Insurance Law Library Edition, §78.02[1].

[66] Subject to restrictions in the NRRA, addressed in section V.C of this Report.

[67] In most instances, laws and regulations that are applicable to "insurers" domiciled in a state apply to licensed "reinsurers" as well unless otherwise specified. See, e.g., N.D. Cent. Code § 26.1-02-05. A reinsurer not offering policies to the public as a primary insurer, for example, would not be subject to approval of its rates and forms.

[68] Comment in response to the FRN on behalf of Tort Trial and Insurance Practice Section of the American Bar Association, 4 (August 27, 2012).

[69] Comment in response to the FRN on behalf of Reinsurance Association of America, 5 (August 27, 2012). Such companies are subject to the applicable supervision of the respective non-U.S. domiciliary jurisdiction.
[70] See, e.g., Iowa Admin. Code r. 191-5.33(510).
[71] See Modernization Report at 37.
[72] 7 U.S.C. § 1501, et seq.
[73] 42 U.S.C. § 2210.
[74] 10 C.F.R. Part 140.
[75] 22 U.S.C. § 2191, et seq.
[76] 49 U.S.C. §§ 44301-10. Authority to provide commercial aviation war risk insurance, other than insurance for aircraft carrying goods or providing services on behalf of the U.S.government, expired on December 11, 2014. 49 U.S.C. 44310. There is a similar program for maritime war risk, administered by the Maritime Administration within the Department of Transportation. 46 U.S.C. §§ 53901-12.
[77] Regarding the NFIP, see Box 2.
[78] 15 U.S.C. § 6701 note.
[79] See The President's Working Group on Financial Markets, The Long-Term Availability and Affordability of Insurance for Terrorism Risk (2014), available at http://www.treasury.gov/initiatives/fio/reports-and-notices.
[80] See 31 C.F.R. Part 223. The Approved Surety list is cross-referenced in other federal programs, e.g., customs bonds. See 19 C.F.R. § 113.37(a).
[81] Subtitle B of title V of the Dodd-Frank Act, 124 Stat. 1595, 15 U.S.C. §§ 8221-8223.
[82] 15 U.S.C. § 8222(a).
[83] Developed following the failure of several large insurers in the 1980's, the NAIC's Financial Regulation Standards and Accreditation Program is a peer review exercise through which state regulators assess whether a state regulatory agency meets a set of legal, financial, and organizational standards. A state insurance regulatory department is "accredited" if it meets these standards. As of December 2013, all fifty states, the District of Columbia and Puerto Rico are accredited. NAIC, Financial Regulation Standards and Accreditation Program (December 2013).
[84] 15 U.S.C. § 8221(a). Similarly, the NRRA also prohibits a state from requiring a reinsurer domiciled in another state to provide any financial information beyond that which the reinsurer is required to file with its domiciliary state. 15 U.S.C. § 8221(b)(1).
[85] In October 2013, Treasury released its 2013 Report on the Impact of Part II of the Nonadmitted and Reinsurance Reform Act in which it found that Part II of the NRRA has not had an adverse impact on the ability of state regulators to access reinsurance information for regulated companies.
[86] 12 U.S.C. § 5323.
[87] 12 U.S.C. §§ 5311(4) (nonbank financial company definitions), 5323 (authority of the Council to determine that a nonbank financial company shall be subject to the supervision of the Board of Governors of the Federal Reserve and enhanced prudential standards); 31 U.S.C. § 313(c)(1)(C) (providing authority to FIO to recommend to the Council that it designate an insurer or an affiliate of an insurer as a nonbank financial company subject to the supervision of the Board of Governors of the Federal Reserve and enhanced prudential standards).
[88] 31 U.S.C. § 313(c)(1)(E). The 56 state-level insurance supervisors, the NAIC and the Board of Governors of the Federal Reserve System also are represented at the IAIS.

[89] Under the current draft of ComFrame, two criteria must be met for an insurance group to be identified as an IAIG: (1) international activity, i.e., the insurance group has premiums written in three or more jurisdictions, and the percentage of gross written premium outside the home jurisdiction is at least 10 percent of the group's total gross written premium; and (2) size, i.e., based on a rolling three-year average, the insurance group has total assets of at least $50 billion or gross written premiums of at least $10 billion. However, involved supervisors have discretion in applying the criteria to determine whether an insurance group qualifies as an IAIG. ComFrame draft and materials available at http://www.iaisweb.org/Supervisory-Material/Common-Framework-765.

[90] See Modernization Report at 23-24. FIO is also participating in work through the IAIS Technical Committee and various subcommittees in the development of a risk-based capital standard that is expected to become part of ComFrame and which, if implemented in a given jurisdiction, would apply at the group level to IAIGs, including reinsurers that are identified as IAIGs.

[91] http://www.financialstabilityboard.org/wp-content/uploads/r_130718.pdf.

[92] http://www.iaisweb.org/view/element_href.cfm?src=1/23741.pdf.

[93] See Testimony of FIO Director Michael T. McRaith before House Financial Services Committee (Nov. 18, 2014), available at http://financialservices.house.gov/uploadedfiles/hhrg-113-ba04-wstate-mmcraith-20141118.pdf.

[94] Information relating to the Project is available at http://www.treasury.gov/initiatives/fio/EU-US%20Insurance%20Project/Pages/default.aspx.

[95] See Modernization Report at 37 (suggesting that such a covered agreement could be based on the NAIC Credit for Reinsurance Model Law and Regulation).

[96] 31 U.S.C. § 313(r)(2).

[97] See section V.D of this Report, further addressing reinsurance collateral reform.

[98] In August 2001, the NAIC Reinsurance Task Force issued a statement generally favoring reduced collateral, but proposing to revisit the issue in another year. In 2003 the NAIC Insolvency Task Force considered but did not recommend establishing an "approved list" of reinsurers approved for reduced collateral. After further consideration of the issue, in 2004 the NAIC Reinsurance Task Force deferred deliberations to permit other interested parties to work on alternatives for regulatory consideration. See National Association of Insurance Commissioners, U.S. Reinsurance Collateral White Paper, 19-21 (March 5, 2006).

[99] Id. at 21.

[100] Id. at 1.

[101] See National Association of Insurance Commissioners, Credit for Reinsurance Model Law & Regulation, ST-785,786.

[102] Id.

[103] By the time the amended Model Law was passed, the NRRA had been enacted as part of the Dodd-Frank Act. The NRRA bars states from denying credit for reinsurance in instances where the state in which the ceding company is licensed has permitted credit for reinsurance.

[104] Modernization Report at 37.

[105] That is, in addition to Florida, New York, New Jersey, and Indiana, which – as noted above – had begun modernizing credit for reinsurance laws and regulations prior to NAIC adoption of the amended Model Law. The number was 18 at the time the Modernization Report was published.

[106] Section VI.B.2.

[107] Modernization Report, 38.

[108] FIO 2014 Annual Report, 46-47.

[109] 31 U.S.C. § 313(f) (permitting FIO's Director to issue a determination that a state insurance law is preempted by a covered agreement, in accordance with certain procedures including providing notice and an opportunity for public comment).

[110] Modernization Report at 1.

[111] SNL Financial, LC.

[112] SNL Financial, LC (cash and invested assets, exclusive of separate account assets held by L/H insurers).

[113] FIO 2014 Annual Report (citing A.M. Best's Aggregates and Averages (2013)).

[114] FIO 2014 Annual Report.

[115] FIO 2014 Annual Report (citing A.M. Best's Aggregates and Averages (2013)). While the L/H sector includes certain accident & health (A/H) coverages, data from firms licensed solely as health insurers or health maintenance organizations are separate and not included in this Report.

[116] FIO 2014 Annual Report.

[117] FIO 2014 Annual Report.

[118] Swiss Re, The Essential Guide to Reinsurance, 12 (2012).

[119] About the Florida Hurricane Catastrophe Fund, available at http://www.sbafla.com/fhcf/AbouttheFHCF/tabid/278/Default.aspx.

[120] Fla. Stat. § 215.555 (1993), as amended.

[121] Representatives of the reinsurance industry have been critical of Florida's approach to addressing the cost and availability of insurance for hurricane risks, as crowding out private market participation. See Comment in response to the FRN on behalf of Reinsurance Association of America, 26 (August 27, 2012). According to recent reports, FHCF has been considering whether to obtain support from private reinsurance markets, although it appears that no such arrangements were in place prior to the 2014 hurricane season.

[122] Further information is available at http://www.earthquakeauthority.com.

[123] CEA recently reported payment of over $212 million in reinsurance premiums. California Earthquake Authority, Annual Report to the Legislature and Insurance Commissioner on CEA Program Operations, 9 (August 2014).

[124] 42 U.S.C. § 4011, et seq.

[125] Public Law 112-141 § 100232, 126 Stat. 916 (2012). To assist in considering the potential role for reinsurance, FEMA is conducting a Flood Insurance Risk Study in furtherance of section 100232(c). See Solicitation Number HSFE60-13-Q-0006.

[126] International Association of Insurance Supervisors, Reinsurance and Financial Stability, 8 (2012).

[127] As shown in Figure 9, a relatively small segment of the reinsurance market relates to "financial" reinsurance which, in this context, includes reinsurance of the following lines: mortgage guarantee, financial guarantee, fidelity, surety, and credit insurance.

[128] International Association of Insurance Supervisors, Reinsurance and Financial Stability, 15 (July 19, 2012).

[129] Current figures are comparatively larger than the 2010 data illustrated in the IAIS exhibit. Annual gross written premium for all direct (primary) lines of insurance is on the order of $4.64 trillion globally. Swiss Re, sigma No. 03/2014: World Insurance in 2013, 35. According to this source, combined U.S. direct premiums written for life, health and property/casualty business in 2013 was on the order of $1.26 trillion. Id. Global reinsurance premiums exceed $220 billion. See A. M. Best, Global Reinsurance – Segment Review: How Relevant is the Underwriting Cycle (Sept. 2014).

[130] Aon Benfield, Reinsurance Market Update (April 1, 2014), available at http://thoughtleadership.aonbenfield.com/Documents/20140401_analytics_reinsurance_market_outlook_april201 4.pdf. Using a narrower definition, broker Guy Carpenter announced that "dedicated sector capital" at year-end 2013 was $322 billion. Guy Carpenter & Co., January 2014 Renewal Report: Capacity: Evolution, Innovation And Opportunity (January 2014), available at http://www.gccapitalideas.com/2014/01/05/january-2014-renewalreport-capacity-evolution-innovation-and-opportunity/.

[131] Press Release, Guy Carpenter & Co., January 1, 2014 Renewals Bring Downward Pressure on Pricing (December 30, 2013); Standard & Poor's Rating Service, "Pricing Slides as Reinsurers Strive for Competitive Footing," in Global Reinsurance Highlights 2014, 18 (2014).

[132] Guy Carpenter Report (Dec. 29, 2013), available at http://www.gccapitalideas.com/2013/12/29/january-1-2014- renewals-bring-downward-pressure-on-pricing/.

[133] Guy Carpenter Report (April 9, 2014), available at http://www.gccapitalideas.com/2014/04/09/april-renewalsbring-price-reductions-focus-on-tailored-coverage/; see also Chubb Benefits from Reinsurers' Pricing Pain During April 1 Renewals (April 25, 2014), available at http://www.snl.com/InteractiveX/article.aspx?ID=27888892&KPLT=4 (" excess supply has driven down prices for certain risks").

[134] Guy Carpenter Report (June 2, 2014), available at http://www. Gccapital ideas.com/2014/06/02/reinsurancepricing-falls-again-at-june-1-2014-as-competition-heightens/; Standard & Poor's Ratings Services, Global Reinsurance Highlights 2014, 13 (2014)

[135] Oliver Suess & Carolyn Bandel, Worst Market in Memory to Weigh on Reinsurance Rates, Bloomberg (September 3, 2014).

[136] E.g., Property Claims Service, PCS Q3 2014 Catastrophe Review(October 2014), available at http://www.verisk.com/pcs/14Q3-Cat-Review.pdf?utm_campaign=&utm_medium=email&utm_source=Eloqua.

[137] Insurance Journal, P/C Reinsurance Market Softer Due to Alternative Capital (March 14, 2014), available at http://www.insurancejournal.com/news/national/2014/03/14/323319.htm (according to Towers Perrin survey, "CFOs attribute this [reinsurance premium] softness primarily to the significant growth of insurance-linked securities [ILS] and other alternative forms of reinsurance capital"). See also Aon Benfield, The Aon Benfield Aggregate – Results for the Full Year Ended December 31, 2013, 5, 8, 19.

[138] See A.M. Best Says Sector Stable, Carrier Management (Jan. 22, 2014) (citing Standard & Poor's Briefing), available at http://www.carriermanagement.com/news/2014/01/22/117972.htm. See also Best's Briefing, Global Re Outlook Remains Stable (Jan. 2, 2014) ("in the supply/demand equation, too much capital chasing the same opportunities has put pressure on reinsurance pricing, terms and conditions"); Carrier Management, Falling Prices Advantage Large Reinsurers, Pressure Smaller Firms (Feb. 27, 2014), available at http://www.carriermanagement.com/news/2014/02/26/119085.htm; Best's Special Report, Could 2013 Be The Apex of the Next Few Years? (April 4, 2014); Standard & Poor's, "Tough Competition Could Put Ratings on Global Reinsurers Under Pressure," in Global Reinsurance Highlights 2014, 62 (2014).

[139] Guy Carpenter Strategic Advisory Update, Reinsurers Ratings Challenged with Negative Sector Outlook (September 15, 2014), available at http://www.gccapitalideas.com/2014/09/15/gc-strategic-advisory-updatereinsurers-ratings-challenged-with-negative-sector-outlook.

[140] Reinsurance Association of America, Reinsurance Underwriting Review: A Financial Review of U.S. Reinsurers, 2013 Industry Results 1, 10 (2014) (based on criteria that include U.S.

reinsurance organizations that have in excess of $10 million of unaffiliated reinsurance premium and $50 million of PHS).

[141] Id. at 1, 3.

[142] Id. at 11.

[143] Reinsurance Association of America, Offshore Reinsurance in the U.S. Market: 2013 Data, 13 (2014). The analysis, based on annual statutory financial statements of licensed U.S. insurers, compares U.S. premiums ceded to U.S. professional reinsurance companies, to the U.S. premiums ceded to non-U.S. reinsurers.

[144] Id at 14. The Reinsurance Association of America states that certain aspects of the U.S. regulatory system have contributed to the observed shift of premiums ceded by U.S. primary insurers from U.S.-based to alien reinsurers. Comment in Response to June 27, 2012 on behalf of Reinsurance Association of America, 8 (August 27, 2012).

[145] Comment in response to the FRN on behalf of Reinsurance Association of America, 9, 17 (August 27, 2012).

[146] David Bruggeman, Results of the 2012 SOA Life Reinsurance Survey, Reinsurance News (Society of Actuaries), Issue 76, 7 (July 2013). Generali U.S. Branch is an affiliate of Assicurazioni Generali, S.p.A., an Italian insurance group.

[147] Id.

[148] Swiss Re, The Essential Guide to Reinsurance, 12 (2013). There are also thousands of small reinsurers, including captives, affiliated, and special purpose reinsurers in 110 jurisdictions worldwide. The vast majority of these companies assume premium from U.S. ceding insurers of less than $10 million annually. Reinsurance Association of America, Offshore Reinsurance in the U.S. Market: 2014 Data, 2-4 and Appendix B, C (2014).

[149] Reinsurance Association of America, Offshore Reinsurance in the U.S. Market: 2013 Data, 4, 6 (2014). In addition, reinsurers in the British Virgin Islands, Ireland, and Barbados assumed between $450 million and $700 million in reinsurance premium, respectively. All figures disregard transactions with affiliated companies.

[150] Standard & Poor's Ratings Services, Global Reinsurance Highlights 2014, 76 (2014).

[151] Id. at 78-95.

[152] J. David Cummins, The Bermuda Insurance Market: An Economic Analysis, 7 (May 6, 2008). Growth of Bermuda as an insurance center expanded following its adoption of Insurance Act 1978, Consolidated Laws of Bermuda.

[153] Deloitte, Bermuda Insurance Market Report 2014, 1 (2014), available at http://www.deloitte.com/assets/DcomBermuda/Local%20Assets/Documents/DELOITTE%20BERMUDA%20INSURANCE%20MARKET%20REPO RT%202014-1.pdf.

[154] Standard & Poor's Ratings Services, Global Reinsurance Highlights 2014, 76 (2014). For a summary of the Bermuda supervisory regime, see International Association of Insurance Supervisors, Reinsurance and Financial Stability, Appendix A1.1 at 37-38 (July 19, 2012).

[155] Deloitte, Bermuda Market Report 2014, 1 (2014). The Market Report tracks 20 Bermuda (re)insurance groups, with total capital and surplus ranging from $529 million to $29 billion.

[156] Deloitte & Standard and Poor's, Bermuda Market Report 2014, 3 - 4 (2014).

[157] Id.

[158] Standard & Poor's Ratings Services, Global Reinsurance Highlights 2014, 76 (2014). This analysis excludes China Reinsurance (Group) Corporation, which both S&P and A.M. Best list as the eighth largest reinsurance group in the world. A.M. Best, Global Reinsurance – Segment Review: How Relevant is the Underwriting Cycle, 13 (September 2014).

[159] Standard & Poor's Ratings Services, Global Reinsurance Highlights 2014, 78-95 (2014).

[160] A.M. Best, Global Reinsurance – Segment Review: How Relevant is the Underwriting Cycle, 19-21(Sept. 2014).

[161] Id.

[162] Bernard Van der Stichele, Some Reflections on the ILS Market from an Institutional Investor Perspective, Alternative Reinsurance Strategies, 258 (2012).

[163] J. David Cummins, The Bermuda Insurance Market: An Economic Analysis, 44 (May 6, 2008).

[164] Bernard Van der Stichele, Some Reflections on the ILS Market from an Institutional Investor Perspective, Alternative Reinsurance Strategies, 260-61 (2012); Angelo John Lewis, What's Behind the Cat Bond Craze (A.M. Best 2014) (advances in catastrophe modeling among factors driving increased cat bond investments and increased used of indemnity triggers in these instruments).

[165] Michael J. Millette, Convergence at High Noon: Catastrophe Risk in the Capital Markets in 2012, 6, in Alternative (Re)insurance Strategies (Morton Lane, ed., 2012).

[166] Id.

[167] A.M. Best Methodology, Rating Natural Catastrophe Bonds, 1 (August 23, 2012).

[168] Id.

[169] Id.

[170] RMS, Cat Bonds Demystified: RMS Guide to the Asset Class, 5-6 (2012).

[171] Marcelo Ramella and Leila Madeiros, Bermuda Sidecars: Supervising Reinsurance Companies in Innovative Global Markets, in The Geneva Papers on Risk and Insurance – Issues and Practice, 349 (2007).

[172] Id. at 351.

[173] Ali Ishaq, Reinsuring for Catastrophes through Industry Loss Warranties – A Practical Approach, Casualty Actuarial Society Forum, 76 (Spring 2005), available at http://www.casact.org/pubs/forum/05spforum/05spf075.pdf.

[174] J. David Cummins, The Bermuda Insurance Market: An Economic Analysis, 44 (May 6, 2008).

[175] Id.

[176] Marcelo Ramella and Leila Madeiros, Bermuda Sidecars: Supervising Reinsurance Companies in Innovative Global Markets, in The Geneva Papers on Risk and Insurance – Issues and Practice, 351-52 (2007).

[177] Ali Ishaq, Reinsuring for Catastrophes through Industry Loss Warranties – A Practical Approach, Casualty Actuarial Society Forum, 4 (Spring 2005), available at http://www.casact.org/pubs/forum/05spforum/05spf075.pdf.

[178] Michael J. Millette, Convergence at High Noon: Catastrophe Risk in the Capital Markets in 2012, 15, in Alternative (Re)insurance Strategies (Morton Lane, ed., 2012).

[179] Standard & Poor's, A Record Volume of Catastrophe Bonds Highlights Increasing Competition in The Insurance-Linked Securities Market, in Global Reinsurance Highlights 2014, 32 (September 2014).

[180] Aon Benfield, Reinsurance Market Update (April 1, 2014), available at http://thoughtleadership.aonbenfield.com/Documents/20140401_analytics_reinsurance_market_outlook_april201 4.pdf. See also Artemis, Insurance-linked Securities Capacity Here to Stay: Hiscox CEO & Chairman (July 21, 2013), available at http://www.artemis.bm/blog/2013/07/31/insurance-linked-securities-capacity-here-to-stay-hiscox-ceo-chairman/ (both the chairman and CEO of Bermuda-based Hiscox group see "insurance-linked securities (ILS) capacity as a permanent and growing feature of the wider insurance and reinsurance market").

[181] Aon Benfield, Insurance-Linked Securities: Evolving Strength 2012, 15 (2012). Note that following 2008, cat bond volumes dipped "due to the higher notional amount of catastrophe bonds reaching maturity … and lower issuance volume following the global financial crisis." Id. at 6.

[182] Id. at 22. Sidecar issuance decreased significantly in 2008 and 2009 before rebounding in 2011. Id.

[183] Aon Benfield, Reinsurance Market Outlook: Post Convergence – The Next USD100 Billion (Sept. 2013), 5. Industry data for this sector are approximate and consist in some measure of estimates, because many of these transactions are private placements and not easily tracked.

[184] A. M. Best's, Third-Party Capital – Industry Implications, in Global Reinsurance – Segment Review (September 2014), 6.

[185] Willis Capital Markets & Advisory, ILS Market Update: Declining Spreads & Flexibility in Structuring (April 2014), available at http://www.willis.com/documents/publications/Services/Capital_Markets/20140407_WCMA_April_ILS_Market _Update.pdf.

[186] Standard & Poor's, A Record Volume of Catastrophe Bonds Highlights Increasing Competition in The Insurance-Linked Securities Market, in Global Reinsurance Highlights 2014, 32 (September 2014).

[187] Carrier Management, Insurance-Linked Securities on Track to Break Issuance Record (October 20, 2014) (based on estimates by Willis Capital Markets & Advisory).

[188] See Swiss Re Obtains USD 275 Million of Extreme Mortality Protection from the Capital Markets through its Vita Programme (July 31, 2012) available at http://www.swissre.com/media/news_releases/nr_120730_extreme_mortality_protection_vita_programme.html; Shankar Ramakrishnan & Joy Wiltermuth, Extreme Mortality Bond Testing Investor View on Pandemic Risk, Reuters (October 20, 2014), available at http://www.reuters.com/article/2014/10/20/mortality-bond-ebolaidUSL2N0SC1E8 201410 20.

[189] See Mark Cobley, Deutsche Agrees Record Longevity Swap Deal, (Feb. 17, 2012), available at http://www.efinancialnews.com/story/2012-02-17/aegon-longevity-swap; Vecta I Ltd. Embedded Value Life Insurance Securitization Completes at C$120m (Dec. 16, 2011), available at http://www.artemis.bm/blog/2011/12/16/vecta-i-ltd-embedded-value-life-securitization-deal-launched/.

[190] "Once the domain of specialty funds narrowly focused on insurance-linked debt, cat bonds have become an alternative for traditional corporate bond managers as they seek higher returns." Wall Street Journal Money Beat, Record "Cat Bond" Grows Again, Cuts Insurer's Costs (April 24, 2014), available at http://blogs.wsj.com/moneybeat/2014/04/24/record-cat-bond-grows-again-cuts-insurers-costs/.

[191] "I think there's a certain amount of complacency out there right now ... there haven't been any significant events in highly cat bond exposed areas, like a Florida cat event." Angelo John Lewis, What's Behind the Cat Bond Craze (A.M. Best 2014) (quoting officer from reinsurance broker, Holborn). See FIO 2014 Annual Report, 32 ("the long term commitment of these non-traditional capital sources has not been tested"); Best's News Service, William R. Berkley Questions "Moral Commitment" of Alternative Capital (October 20, 2014).

[192] 31 U.S.C. § 313(o)(1).

Index

#

A

B

C

D

E

F

G

H

I

J

K

L

M

N

O

P

Q

R

S

T

U

V

W

Y